THE
SEMINOLE

THE
SEMINOLE

Merwyn S. Garbarino
The University of Illinois at Chicago

Frank W. Porter III
General Editor

CHELSEA HOUSE PUBLISHERS
New York   Philadelphia

On the cover Seminole palmetto fiber
dolls dressed in patchwork garments
characteristic of the Indians of
Southern Florida.

Chelsea House Publishers
Editor-in-Chief   Nancy Toff
Executive Editor   Remmel T. Nunn
Managing Editor   Karyn Gullen Browne
Copy Chief   Juliann Barbato
Picture Editor   Adrian G. Allen
Manufacturing Manager   Gerald Levine

Indians of North America
Senior Editor   Marjorie P. K. Weiser

Staff for **THE SEMINOLE**
Associate Editor   Andrea E. Reynolds
Assistant Editor   Karen Schimmel
Copy Editor   David Waldstreicher
Deputy Copy Chief   Ellen Scordato
Editorial Assistant   Tara P. Deal
Assistant Art Director   Laurie Jewell
Designer   Victoria Tomaselli
Picture Researchers   Alan Gottlieb, Ann Levy
Production Coordinator   Joseph Romano

5 7 9 8 6 4

Library of Congress Cataloging in Publication Data

Garbarino, Merwyn S.
The Seminole / Merwyn S. Garbarino
  p. cm.—(Indians of North America)
Bibliography: p.
Includes index.
Summary: Examines the culture, history, and changing
fortunes of the Seminole Indians. Includes a color section on
their crafts.
ISBN 1-55546-729-6
  0-7910-0367-1 (pbk.)
1. Seminole Indians. [1. Seminole Indians. 2. Indians of North
America.] I. Title. II. Series: Indians of North America
(Chelsea House Publishers)   88-5103
E99.S28G33   1988   CIP
973'.0497—dc 19   AC

CONTENTS

INDIANS OF NORTH AMERICA

CHELSEA HOUSE PUBLISHERS

INDIANS OF NORTH AMERICA: CONFLICT AND SURVIVAL

Frank W. Porter III

*The Indians survived our
open intention of wiping them
out, and since the tide turned
they have even weathered
our good intentions toward them,
which can be much more deadly.*

John Steinbeck
America and Americans

When Europeans first reached the North American continent, they found hundreds of tribes occupying a vast and rich country. The newcomers quickly recognized the wealth of natural resources. They were not, however, so quick or willing to recognize the spiritual, cultural, and intellectual riches of the people they called Indians.

The Indians of North America examines the problems that develop when people with different cultures come together. For American Indians, the consequences of their interaction with non-Indian people have been both productive and tragic. The Europeans believed they had "discovered" a "New World," but their religious bigotry, cultural bias, and materialistic world view kept them from appreciating and understanding the people who lived in it. All too often they attempted to change the way of life of the indigenous people. The Spanish conquistadores wanted the Indians as a source of labor. The Christian missionaries, many of whom were English, viewed them as potential converts. French traders and trappers used the Indians as a means to obtain pelts. As Francis Parkman, the 19th-century historian, stated, "Spanish civilization crushed the Indian; English civilization scorned and neglected him; French civilization embraced and cherished him."

Nearly 500 years later, many people think of American Indians as curious vestiges of a distant past, waging a futile war to survive in a Space Age society. Even today, our understanding of the history and culture of American Indians is too often derived from unsympathetic, culturally biased, and inaccurate reports. The American Indian, described and portrayed in thousands of movies, television programs, books, articles, and government studies, has either been raised to the status of the "noble savage" or disparaged as the "wild Indian" who resisted the westward expansion of the American frontier.

7

Where in this popular view are the real Indians, the human beings and communities whose ancestors can be traced back to ice-age hunters? Where are the creative and indomitable people whose sophisticated technologies used the natural resources to ensure their survival, whose military skill might even have prevented European settlement of North America if not for devastating epidemics and the disruption of the ecology? Where are the men and women who are today diligently struggling to assert their legal rights and express once again the value of their heritage?

The various Indian tribes of North America, like people everywhere, have a history that includes population expansion, adaptation to a range of regional environments, trade across wide networks, internal strife, and warfare. This was the reality. Europeans justified their conquests, however, by creating a mythical image of the New World and its native people. In this myth, the New World was a virgin land, waiting for the Europeans. The arrival of Christopher Columbus ended a timeless primitiveness for the original inhabitants.

Also part of this myth was the debate over the origins of the American Indians. Fantastic and diverse answers were proposed by the early explorers, missionaries, and settlers. Some thought that the Indians were descended from the Ten Lost Tribes of Israel, others that they were descended from inhabitants of the lost continent of Atlantis. One writer suggested that the Indians had reached North America in another Noah's ark.

A later myth, perpetrated by many historians, focused on the relentless persecution during the past five centuries until only a scattering of these ''primitive'' people remained to be herded onto reservations. This view fails to chronicle the overt and covert ways in which the Indians successfully coped with the intruders.

All of these myths presented one-sided interpretations that ignored the complexity of European and American events and policies. All left serious questions unanswered. What were the origins of the American Indians? Where did they come from? How and when did they get to the New World? What was their life—their culture—really like?

In the late 1800s, anthropologists and archaeologists in the Smithsonian Institution's newly created Bureau of American Ethnology in Washington, D. C., began to study scientifically the history and culture of the Indians of North America. They were motivated by an honest belief that the Indians were on the verge of extinction and that along with them would vanish their languages, religious beliefs, technology, myths, and legends. These men and women went out to visit, study, and record data from as many Indian communities as possible before this information was forever lost.

By this time there was a new myth in the national consciousness. American Indians existed as figures in the American past. They had performed a historical mission. They had challenged white settlers who trekked across the continent. Once conquered, however, they were supposed to accept graciously the way of life of their conquerors.

The reality again was different. American Indians resisted both actively and passively. They refused to lose their unique identity, to be assimilated into white society. Many whites viewed the Indians not only as members of a conquered nation but also as "inferior" and "unequal." The rights of the Indians could be expanded, contracted, or modified as the conquerors saw fit. In every generation, white society asked itself what to do with the American Indians. Their answers have resulted in the twists and turns of federal Indian policy.

There were two general approaches. One way was to raise the Indians to a "higher level" by "civilizing" them. Zealous missionaries considered it their Christian duty to elevate the Indian through conversion and scanty education. The other approach was to ignore the Indians until they disappeared under pressure from the ever-expanding white society. The myth of the "vanishing Indian" gave stronger support to the latter option, helping to justify the taking of the Indians' land.

Prior to the end of the 18th century, there was no national policy on Indians simply because the American nation had not yet come into existence. American Indians similarly did not possess a political or social unity with which to confront the various Europeans. They were not homogeneous. Rather, they were loosely formed bands and tribes, speaking nearly 300 languages and thousands of dialects. The collective identity felt by Indians today is a result of their common experiences of defeat and/or mistreatment at the hands of whites.

During the colonial period, the British crown did not have a coordinated policy toward the Indians of North America. Specific tribes (most notably the Iroquois and the Cherokee) became military and political pawns used by both the crown and the individual colonies. The success of the American Revolution brought no immediate change. When the United States acquired new territory from France and Mexico in the early 19th century, the federal government wanted to open this land to settlement by homesteaders. But the Indian tribes that lived on this land had signed treaties with European governments assuring their title to the land. Now the United States assumed legal responsibility for honoring these treaties.

At first, President Thomas Jefferson believed that the Louisiana Purchase contained sufficient land for both the Indians and the white population.

Within a generation, though, it became clear that the Indians would not be allowed to remain. In the 1830s the federal government began to coerce the eastern tribes to sign treaties agreeing to relinquish their ancestral land and move west of the Mississippi River. Whenever these negotiations failed, President Andrew Jackson used the military to remove the Indians. The southeastern tribes, promised food and transportation during their removal to the West, were instead forced to walk the "Trail of Tears." More than 4,000 men, women, and children died during this forced march. The "removal policy" was successful in opening the land to homesteaders, but it created enormous hardships for the Indians.

By 1871 most of the tribes in the United States had signed treaties ceding most or all of their ancestral land in exchange for reservations and welfare. The treaty terms were intended to bind both parties for all time. But in the General Allotment Act of 1887, the federal government changed its policy again. Now the goal was to make tribal members into individual landowners and farmers, encouraging their absorption into white society. This policy was advantageous to whites who were eager to acquire Indian land, but it proved disastrous for the Indians. One hundred thirty-eight million acres of reservation land were subdivided into tracts of 160, 80, or as little as 40 acres, and allotted to tribe members on an individual basis. Land owned in this way was said to have "trust status" and could not be sold. But the surplus land—all Indian land not allotted to individuals— was opened (for sale) to white settlers. Ultimately, more than 90 million acres of land were taken from the Indians by legal and illegal means.

The resulting loss of land was a catastrophe for the Indians. It was necessary to make it illegal for Indians to sell their land to non-Indians. The Indian Reorganization Act of 1934 officially ended the allotment period. Tribes that voted to accept the provisions of this act were reorganized, and an effort was made to purchase land within preexisting reservations to restore an adequate land base.

Ten years later, in 1944, federal Indian policy again shifted. Now the federal government wanted to get out of the "Indian business." In 1953 an act of Congress named specific tribes whose trust status was to be ended "at the earliest possible time." This new law enabled the United States to end unilaterally, whether the Indians wished it or not, the special status that protected the land in Indian tribal reservations. In the 1950s federal Indian policy was to transfer federal responsibility and jurisdiction to state governments, encourage the physical relocation of Indian peoples from reservations to urban areas, and hasten the termination, or extinction, of tribes.

Between 1954 and 1962 Congress passed specific laws authorizing the termination of more than 100 tribal groups. The stated purpose of the termination policy was to ensure the full and complete integration of Indians into American society. However, there is a less benign way to interpret this legislation. Even as termination was being discussed in Congress, 133 separate bills were introduced to permit the transfer of trust land ownership from Indians to non-Indians.

With the Johnson administration in the 1960s the federal government began to reject termination. In the 1970s yet another Indian policy emerged. Known as "self-determination," it favored keeping the protective role of the federal government while increasing tribal participation in, and control of, important areas of local government. In 1983 President Reagan, in a policy statement on Indian affairs, restated the unique "government to government" relationship of the United States with the Indians. However, federal programs since then have moved toward transferring Indian affairs to individual states, which have long desired to gain control of Indian land and resources.

As long as American Indians retain power, land, and resources that are coveted by the states and the federal government, there will continue to be a "clash of cultures," and the issues will be contested in the courts, Congress, the White House, and even in the international human rights community. To give all Americans a greater comprehension of the issues and conflicts involving American Indians today is a major goal of this series. These issues are not easily understood, nor can these conflicts be readily resolved. The study of North American Indian history and culture is a necessary and important step toward that comprehension. All Americans must learn the history of the relations between the Indians and the federal government, recognize the unique legal status of the Indians, and understand the heritage and cultures of the Indians of North America.

Chief of a Florida tribe, drawn by the English colonist John White around 1585.

THE
WAY THEY
WERE

As the United States is a nation made up of people from many nations, so the Seminole is a tribe made up of Indians from many tribes. In the early 18th century, many tribes lived in southeastern North America, in what are now the states of Georgia, Alabama, North Carolina, South Carolina, Tennessee, and Mississippi. These Indians all came under pressure from Europeans to give up their lands for settlement by non-Indians. Some fled south into the Spanish territory of Florida. The nucleus of this group was a band of Creek Indians. They were later joined by members of other tribes and became known as the Seminole.

The Indians who sought refuge in Florida all had similar ways of life, or cultures. Even after they moved, they retained many characteristics of their original culture. This general southeastern culture represents the traditions of the Seminole forefathers.

Among the Indian tribes the Europeans found living in the Southeast were the Creek, Choctaw, Chickasaw, Cherokee, Yuchi, Yamassee, Apalachicola, Timucua, and Calusa. Sixteenth-century Spanish explorers wrote about the southeastern Indians. They described them as tall people whose complexions ranged from olive to brownish. Indians in the cloudier, colder mountain areas were usually described as having lighter skin tone; those who lived in sunnier regions appeared to have been tanned to a ruddier and browner hue.

The natural environment affected every aspect of the Indians' life. It determined the food they ate, the clothing they wore, and the houses they built and lived in. The natural environment also affected their language and influenced their rituals. Because their lives were so closely involved with the natural world they lived in, they had great reverence for all things of that world—animals, plants, air, rain, sunshine, waterways, and the earth itself.

The southeastern landscape was made up of fertile valleys, thick woods, and low mountains. The largest and

Maize, or Indian corn, in a drawing from the Histoire naturelle des Indes, *published about 1590. Of the three primary crops the Indians grew, corn was the most important.*

most powerful tribes settled in the most desirable locations, the river valleys, which flooded regularly. The soil there was rich and easily worked. The smaller tribes settled in the woods and mountains, where the soil was not as fertile but where food was still readily available in the form of plentiful wildlife, especially small game animals.

The most important influence of the environment on the Indians' life was in determining the types of food the people could find. Before Europeans arrived, most of the southeastern Indians practiced horticulture (farming with simple hand implements), tending gardens of maize (corn), beans, and squash. These crops were so important

to the Indians' diet that they are sometimes called the trinity of American Indian agriculture. The Indians also obtained some of their food through hunting and fishing. The woodlands and rivers were filled with an abundance of game that provided the people with a varied diet. In addition the Indians gathered plant foods that they found in the environment, including berries, nuts, tubers, and seeds.

Before the Europeans arrived, there were two major tribes living in what is now the state of Florida. The Timucua, a populous, settled people with many villages, lived in northern Florida. Like most of the southeastern Indians, they were horticulturists. The Calusa and their neighbors in southern Florida, however, relied entirely on hunting, fishing, and gathering wild plant foods from their surroundings. The growing season in southern Florida was long, and plant foods were available nearly year-round.

Among the Timucua and the Calusa, as within all southeastern Indian societies, the tasks of gathering and growing were women's work. The men helped out when there was heavy and intensive work to be done, such as clearing land and harvesting, but their primary tasks were hunting, fishing, and warfare. The first Europeans to observe the Indians were surprised at the constant work expected of Indian women and thought the men were lazy. The Indians themselves, however, did not regard their division of labor as inequitable. Although men's work may

The southeastern Indians stretched and dried animal skins on a frame made of tree limbs. A sketch from the Fifth Annual Report *of the Bureau of American Ethnology, 1887.*

have been less constant, it was far from easy. Hunting was demanding and rigorous, and there was no guarantee of success. Men's responsibilities to protect the community from raids by other Indians also required periods of great physical stress and endurance.

The men hunted animals for both their meat and their hides. The deer was the most important animal, not only because of its prime meat but also because of its large, smooth hide, which the women tanned into leather for clothing. The men also hunted squirrels, rabbits, racoons, and bears. They used the furry hide of the bear for cloth-

ing and the fat for cooking, as well as for dressing their hair and oiling their skin. Indian men and women liked the glossy appearance bear fat gave to their hair and skin. Turkeys, ducks, and geese were also plentiful and were popular foods among the southeastern Indians.

In areas where alligators were found, Indians hunted them for their meat. To immobilize the jaws of the reptiles, they thrusted heavy spears into their mouths. Indians also ate turtle meat and shellfish where they were available, and both fresh- and saltwater fish of many varieties.

Men used a variety of hunting and fishing equipment. Hunting large game required bows and arrows, spears, and stone knives. The hunters used blowguns to kill small animals and birds. From hardwood they fashioned darts measuring 15 to 20 inches long and placed these sharp projectiles at one end of a hollowed-out cane about 8 feet long. The darts were held in place by a wadding of vegetable fiber or animal hair that sealed the gun. When a person blew through the hollow tube against the resistance of the wadding, the dart was ejected. Some Indians became so proficient in the use of blowguns that their aim was accurate up to 50 feet.

Each hunter made his own equipment, although sometimes the men traded weapons with one another. Young boys learned to make their equipment by first imitating adult weapons for play and then by studying under the guidance of an older male.

The men often hunted in groups. They would drive deer into prepared surrounds, or corrals, by setting fire to

This 1591 engraving, based on a painting by the French colonist Jacques Le Moyne, depicts Timucua Indians hunting alligators.

the woods. Then they shot the trapped animals with bows and arrows. Sometimes groups of hunters would disguise themselves by wearing deerskins with the heads and antlers still attached. This way they could approach a herd of deer without frightening them.

For catching fish, the men used hooks and lines, nets, and gorges, sharp pieces of wood or bone tied to a line. These small fragments would become lodged in a fish's throat, immobilizing the fish. The men carved fishing hooks out of antler, bone, or shell and fashioned lines and nets from the inner bark of trees or spun vegetable fibers or animal hair. In some areas, a poison was also used to disable the fish without harming the eater. Fish stupefied by the poison could be lifted from the water by hand. This method could be used only in still pools, not in running water, which dissipated the poison. The Indians also constructed weirs, or fish traps, made of woven branches, reeds, or loosely piled rocks to block a river or stream. Water flowed through the cracks in the weir, but fish, too large to pass through, would be trapped and held safely until collected. The men could often catch the blocked fish with their hands.

The women were responsible for preparing and cooking the food the men obtained. They baked, boiled, or broiled it, often adding vegetables to the boiled meat to create a stew. They thickened the stew with cornmeal and seasoned it with wild plant foods such

Arrowheads found near St. Augustine, dating from 2,000–500 B.C. They were made of a type of flint known as chert.

as garlic or onion or sweetened it with maple sugar. The women preserved foods they collected, such as plums and persimmons, as well as some vegetables they grew, by drying them. They also boiled, baked, or pounded into flour various tubers and roots they found in the surrounding environment.

Nothing in the Indian diet was more important than maize, which the

A rectangular clay vessel used by the Indians of Florida. The design was scratched into the surface while the clay was still wet.

women prepared in many ways. They made a drink or chowder out of it by roasting the ears to separate the corn from the cob and then pounding the kernels and boiling them to a liquid consistency. From dried corn, they made cornmeal by soaking and softening the dried kernels and pounding them into a fine meal. They used the meal for baking or to thicken stews. Added to liquid, it became a porridge. Some was stored for later use or carried by travelers to eat on their journey. A thick batter of cornmeal and water was wrapped in corn husks and boiled to make a kind of bread. The women might add nuts, sunflower seeds, or boiled beans to the various corn dishes they prepared.

The dish the Indians preferred most, however, was hominy. It was made by mixing corn kernels with wood ashes and soaking the mixture overnight. Soaking the corn loosened the hulls, the outer covering of the kernels. The women then pounded the corn to remove the hulls and cooked the kernels in water for several hours. The result was thinned with water, mashed, and made into a drink or boiled with meat to be eaten as a stew.

The women used a wide range of equipment to aid them in preparing food. They pounded corn, seeds, and other plants in a hollowed tree trunk or log to make meal or flour. The food was placed inside, and using a heavy wooden pole that served as a pestle, the women hammered or pounded it to the desired consistency.

Food was stored in baskets the women made from cane, reeds, or other materials from the environment. The women also used baskets for gathering and carrying wild plant foods. A well-made basket was strong and light, adding little to the burden on the return trip when it held a full load of berries or other foods. Flat, traylike baskets served as sifters to remove the hulls from corn and seeds.

The women also made pottery for use in cooking, eating, and storage.

Dried gourds that had been hollowed out served as containers, ladles, and cups. The men carved large wooden spoons, which were used not as eating utensils but as ladles for serving food. (After the arrival of Europeans, who introduced metal utensils to the Indians, implements made of metal would eventually replace ones made of wood, and many of the traditional ways of making these objects would be forgotten.)

To clear fields for farming, the men usually set fire to a wooded area rather than cut the trees down. The best land was found in the river valleys, the area where floods annually deposited fertile silt. The land was rich and easily worked, with few rocks. The women planted the crops in small gardens close

A Choctaw pipe bowl made of clay. When in use, the bowl was attached to a stem made from hollow reed or cane.

to their homes and in larger communal fields. The communal fields were for the entire village, and everyone participated in cultivating the land. A portion of the produce from these fields went to the chief for his use and also for storage as a reserve against difficult times.

The Indians' primary crops—corn, beans, and squash—grew well in the same field. First the women planted corn kernels in small hills. They made several holes in each hill and placed the kernels into the holes. Then they covered the kernels with soil. After the corn sprouted, weak plants were thinned out. The women then planted beans so that the vines could wind around the corn stalks as they grew. They also planted squashes among the corn hills, and sometimes sunflowers.

Cultivation was minimal. The women weeded and kept the corn hill built up for good drainage. They had only one tool, a simple pointed digging stick, which they used for planting and weeding. Sometimes children helped scare the birds away from the fields. When the crops ripened, the women and men worked together to bring in the harvest. The food was stored for the winter in containers that were raised off the ground and lined inside and out with clay mud that had been allowed to dry. This kept it safe from rodents and vermin.

The Indians also grew tobacco. Both men and women smoked. The men fashioned pipes out of the stems of hollow reeds or cane, at one end of which they attached a clay bowl. The Indians smoked for pleasure and for ceremonial and religious purposes. Smoking was considered a gesture of peace and good will. Tobacco was used as a medicine; the variety grown was very strong and probably had a narcotic effect. It also suppressed hunger. Generally, the Indians smoked a mixture of dried tobacco leaves and the dried leaves of other plants, usually sumac, although they sometimes used sweetgum leaves. This tobacco mixture was called *kinnikinnick* by the Algonquian-speaking Indians of northeastern North America.

Most of the peoples of the Southeast spoke Muskhogean languages. Speakers of one Muskhogean language could not understand speakers of another, just as speakers of English are unable to understand German, although they are from the same family of languages. Other Indians in the area spoke Siouan and Algonquian languages.

The Indians of the Southeast lived in villages that ranged in size from 20 to 100 houses and in population from 100 to more than 1,000 inhabitants. Usually homes were built around a square or town plaza, but sometimes they were scattered along a river or creek. If the village had a public square, the central area was usually left open for ceremonial purposes. The village chief's house, a council house or meeting hall, a storage building, and often the house of an important medicine man or religious leader surrounded the square. Around these buildings, the townspeople built their living quarters.

Individual families constructed summer and winter houses, as well as separate buildings for storage and cooking and a special residence for a mother and her newborn baby. These buildings were usually clustered around a small central space, duplicating the format of the town square.

Men built the houses from whatever materials were available in the region. The structures, usually round or rectangular in shape, had a framework of tree trunks entwined with reeds or branches. The sides of the summer houses were usually left open or loosely woven with branches to allow maximum air flow. Winter houses were similar but more tightly constructed and insulated on the outside with packed clay. Both summer and winter dwellings had thatched roofs made of grasses, branches, leaves, or bark.

The baby house, a smaller version of the summer or winter house, was where a woman traditionally gave birth. She and her newborn remained in the house until the baby was four months old. During these months, she was considered polluted or dangerous to men, and all men carefully avoided contact with her, for they believed it would make them ill. While the woman was in the baby house, she prepared her own food. After the four months had passed, the woman returned with her baby to her family house, and they became a part of the household.

Some of the towns were stockaded or palisaded, surrounded with logs that were sunk into the ground to form a protective fence. There would be one or two openings in the walls to allow passage in and out, and several smaller openings were left to enable the warriors to shoot arrows in defense. Sometimes the men reinforced the poles with crossbeams and daubed clay or mud over the cracks and open spaces.

There was little sense of unity or tribal cohesion between the various villages, even if their people spoke the same language. Villages formed loose alliances, often participating together in ceremonies, and they recognized each other as friends, but they did not necessarily join each other in taking hostile actions against other villages. Nor did they recognize any one leader or chief of the entire linguistic group. The individual village was truly the important and independent unit of decision making.

The Indians of the Southeast belonged to clans. Within most southeastern Indian societies, every person was, from birth, a member of the clan to which his or her mother belonged.

A palisaded Indian village, shown in a 1591 engraving.

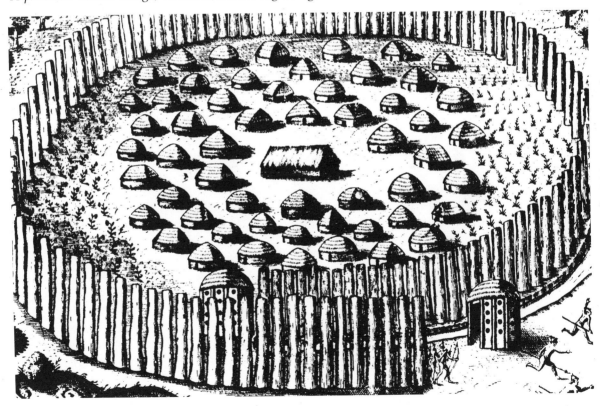

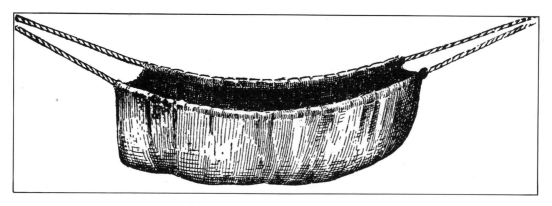

A baby hammock, or cradle, used by the Indians of Florida. Very young babies were placed in hammocks, older ones on a deerskin or on the warm ground. This drawing appeared in the Fifth Annual Report *of the Bureau of American Ethnology, 1887.*

Clan membership was as important as the village a person lived in and the tribe he or she belonged to. Clans were ranked within some tribes, so that one clan was considered distinctly superior or more prestigious than another.

A clan was responsible for the welfare of its members. Because a boy did not belong to his father's clan, one of his mother's brothers (maternal uncles), or one of her cousins if she had no brothers, was the primary person responsible for instructing the boy in hunting and warfare. Girls, too, were the responsibility of their clan. Because they learned women's tasks from their mother, who was also of their clan, girls were less exposed to guidance from their uncles. Although a father was responsible for the support of his children and almost always had a warm relationship with them, they did not belong to his clan. Every man's first responsibility was to the children of his sister, who were members of his own clan.

The maternal uncle was also responsible for punishing bad behavior. Occasionally punishment took the form of flogging, but most often an offender, child or adult, was subjected to dry scratching. A mother, maternal uncle, or other member of the clan used a wooden implement embedded with garfish teeth or splinters of bone to scratch the skin of anyone who misbehaved. The resulting scratch marks were more humiliating than painful, as they were a visible symbol of misbehavior and punishment. The transgressor was shamed before all society.

A person had to marry someone who belonged to a different clan. It was also unusual for a person to marry someone from his or her father's clan, although such marriages were not absolutely forbidden, as marriages within one's own clan were. Because a marriage created an alliance between clans, it was almost as important to the clan's members as to the couple themselves.

Older clan kin arranged marriages for young people that they deemed suitable, being careful that the couple did not come from forbidden clans—linked clans whose members were considered to be brothers and sisters. The elders of the young man's clan would discuss the possibility of marriage with the elders of the young woman's clan. Sometimes marriages were arranged without consulting the couple, or at least without consulting the woman, but after the elders were satisfied with preliminary arrangements the two young people still had to give their consent. No one was forced to marry.

In arranging a match, the elders also considered the candidate's potential. A good husband was a good provider, and a good wife was a good manager of domestic chores. When both the clan elders and young people agreed to the match, the young man gave gifts to the bride-to-be's relatives to indicate his serious intentions and to repay them in advance for losing her help in their household. The gifts also indicated the man's maturity and sense of responsibility in the new relationship and in the demands of providing for a family.

After the gifts were accepted by the bride's relatives, the couple usually went through some type of ceremony, often a feast. They could, however, set up housekeeping without a ceremony. In most cases, southeastern Indian societies were matrilocal, which meant that the couple lived with or near the bride's mother. The new husband built a house and in time added other buildings around it. He also cleared the fields for his wife to cultivate. The houses and fields were thought of as clan property and usually belonged to the women.

A man of very high status—a renowned warrior or skilled hunter who could supply more food and hides than one woman could reasonably manage—might take a second wife. In most southeastern tribes this could be done only with the agreement of the first wife, who remained the principal wife. Very few men ever had more than two wives. Second and later wives were usually sisters or maternal cousins of the first wife, and thus members of her clan. The husband built a separate house for each wife, which helped maintain harmony in the household. These later wives assisted with the work, and the first wife was usually glad to have them. Her position was secure as the dominant wife. Most of the women who shared a husband did not object because the arrangement was a symbol of high status, and all the wives participated in the growing prominence of their husband.

Among most southeastern people, divorce was a mere matter of separation. If a woman wanted a divorce, she indicated that the man should leave by placing a bundle of his belongings outside the house. If the man wanted a divorce, he simply left. Because all property, except for personal items such as clothing and tools, belonged to the woman and was inherited through clan lines, a divorced man moved back into his mother's house. If the man had more than one wife, he might move into the home of another wife, as each wife had her own house. A divorced man would continue to see his children and was responsible for supporting them. The clans' members always made sure that fathers lived up to their responsibilities in caring for their children.

In addition to their significant role in regard to marriage and property, clans had important ceremonial and political responsibilities. Each village and tribe had some kind of civil organization, or government, that was headed by a civil leader or chief. The chief made decisions concerning public matters such as food storage, feasts, public works, and communal agricultural activities. Frequently the position of civil chief was hereditary to one clan. Leaders would be selected from among the males of a specific clan based on their competence and experience.

The civil leader was assisted by advisers and a council of leading warriors and respected elders. Although military strategy was usually left to a war chief, the civil chief often participated in decisions to go to war or to seek peace. On issues of great importance the civil chief and council did not act on their own accord but almost always sought a general consensus of the people.

Each village usually had a head war chief who was responsible for planning and overseeing military maneuvers once the decision to go to war was made. A war chief was always a proven warrior, someone others would follow.

He was not elected to the position but recognized by the people as the most able leader. The head war chief would ordinarily lead the larger expeditions, although another individual might try to persuade other warriors to join him in a smaller war party.

Warfare was the way to glory and prestige for a man. From childhood, when a boy would play at being a warrior, to his early experiences as a very junior member of a war party, a man sought distinction through bravery and daring. The warrior who returned home with trophies of scalps or captives—usually taken by swift attack and, it was hoped, speedy return—gained status among the tribe. Those men who attained war honors and retired from warfare were assured a place on the village council. To show their eminence, warriors wore feathers, most commonly eagle feathers, on their clothing and in their hair. They also painted and tattooed their bodies. Although both men and women tattooed their skin, men especially displayed elaborate designs over most of their bodies. In addition to being decorative and a sign of distinction in battle, tattoos indicated social and political standing, a kind of badge or insignia of office and social status.

Although warfare was frequent, it was usually done on a small scale. It was carried on for revenge, renown, or captives, not for territory. Sometimes captives, particularly women and children, were kept as slaves, but male captives were usually put to death, frequently after being tortured. Slavery did not necessarily mean a difficult life for the captive. Although not physically cruel, slavery was considered shameful, and slaves had no political rights and the lowest social standing. Nonetheless, captors sometimes adopted their captives and treated them like any other kinfolk. Children born to slave women were usually free. They lived with their mother and still belonged to her clan, which often had members in the village in which she was held captive.

Each member of a war party was responsible for making and carrying his own weapons, which included a bow and arrows, a knife, and a war club. Warriors also had to bring their own provisions, usually cornbread or dried corn that could be cooked with water and eaten while away from home. The entire war party had to be acceptable to the supernatural world, so before setting out the warriors performed various

Politically or socially prominent people traveled in litters made from tree saplings. This engraving of the wife of a Timucua chief appeared in Indorum Floridam provinciam inhabitantium eicones, *a book of engravings by Theodore De Bry published in 1591.*

rituals that almost always included purification ceremonies such as fasting and sweating. Warriors returning from battle were considered polluted, and they would sweat to become pure once more.

For purification by sweating, men built sweathouses—small, tightly constructed buildings near rivers or streams. The sweathouse was heated with hot stones, and sometimes water was sprinkled on the stones to create steam. The opening to the house was closed off. After about an hour, when the warrior was sweating profusely, he left the sweathouse and plunged into the running water nearby. Indians believed this ritual purified and strengthened the participant and increased his agility as well. They also used sweating to cure fever and soothe aches and pains.

People and their belongings traveled long distances in bark canoes and dugouts. Dugouts were the most common means of transportation. These boats could be made from several kinds of wood, but the men preferred to use cypress because it was readily available, easy to work, and buoyant. Once they found a suitable tree, the men felled it by burning the base and chipping away at it with stone axes. The tree was then carried to a clearing and placed in a horizontal position. The men built a fire on it, carefully controlling the blaze so it would not burn too much at a time. They scraped away the charred wood with axes and little by little carved out the log. When the canoe was suitably

hollowed out, the men shaped the outside using axes and adzes, hoelike tools that could strike at right angles. The canoes, some of which measured 40 to 50 feet long, were propelled by paddles or poles. Some early European explorers reported that Indians traveled as far away as Cuba by canoe.

For overland travel, the Indians went on foot, carrying their possessions in a backpack made of hide. Important older people or those of special political or ceremonial importance were transported in litters that were carried on the shoulders of four or more men. The litters were fashioned from two strong saplings, with hides or tree limbs placed across them. Sometimes a shade of branches protected the riders.

Indians throughout the Southeast wore clothing made of leather. The standard dress for men was the loin cloth, which was made from a long strip of leather that was passed between the legs and held in place at the waist with a leather thong or belt of twined plant fibers. In the winter and when traveling, men added leggings, which protected their legs from the cold and from being scratched by underbrush. The leggings were fashioned from two tube-shaped pieces of leather. Each piece enclosed a leg and was held in place by a garter. In very cold weather the men might also wear fur robes, usually made of bearskin, although rabbit, marten, and wildcat were used as well.

Women wore apronlike skirts that hung down to the thighs or knees. They were made from two pieces of leather

Seminole man's leggings made of deerskin and trimmed with fringe. Both men and women wore leggings for warmth and protection.

that were held in place at the waist or under the arms with a thong or belt. In the winter, women wore longer skirts and added leggings and fur robes. They wove cloth from the fibrous inner bark of the mulberry tree and used the material for shawls and blankets. Other plant fibers native to the Southeast were occasionally woven into cloth and used for skirts or capes. Sometimes the women combined animal hair with the plant fibers before weaving the cloth.

Young children usually went without clothes in warm weather, and most southeastern Indians did not wear anything on their feet except in cold weather or for travel. When footwear was required, the Indians wore deerskin or bearskin moccasins.

Leather made from deerskin was the most common material used for clothing. Men usually skinned the animals, but women usually prepared the leather. The women scraped the hair off the skin and then tanned it by soaking it for several hours in a solution of water and mashed animal brains. Afterward they stretched and kneaded the skins until they were soft and pliable. The tanner might then smoke the piece, which turned it a darker color. The end product was a soft hide that could be used for many purposes. When several skins were needed to make a larger garment, the women sewed the pieces together with leather thongs.

The Indians used a wide variety of feathers for decoration. Feathers were a sign of social prominence, and people of high status, both men and women, occasionally wore feathered capes. The most common type of feathers the Indians used were those of the turkey, but the most sought-after and highly prized feathers were those of the eagle.

Leather bags or pouches were used to hold tobacco, pipes, and other possessions. The Indians decorated the straps of these bags, as well as belts, garters, and moccasins, with beads made from shells. Belts made of shells were used as as a medium of exchange or kind of money. Europeans called shell beads wampum, from the Alqonquian word *wampumpeag*. Men and women wore earrings, necklaces, and pendants made of shell, bone, pearls, and animal claws, especially bear claws. Soon after European contact, the Indians began to make jewelry from metal obtained in trade. They particularly liked European coins, which they hammered into thin disks and suspended from strings of shell beads.

Warriors, curers, and religious specialists owned bags made of pelts or fiber in which they carried both practical and sacred articles. A warrior might carry such a pouch on the trail or into battle. The bag would contain cornmeal or cornbread as well as an assortment of items that symbolized the presence of his spirit protector. Warriors believed such items, sacred to the owners, would not only protect them but also give them strength and good fortune. A curer or religious specialist might carry a bag containing herbs for curing and charms for contacting the supernatural world. There were many different charms and sacred items because specific objects were symbolic to an individual and usually meaningless to others. Such an item might be a beautiful or unusual stone, a feather, beads, pearls, or an animal's claw. Because the items contained in a pouch held special powers for the owner, they were often referred to as his "medicine," and the pouches that held them were called medicine bags. Almost all Indians carried tobacco in their medicine bags because it was believed to have curative as well as sacred power.

The southeastern Indians thought their world was occupied by a multitude of beings—humans and nonhu-mans—including dwarfs, giants, ogres, and souls, as well as the spirits of animals, plants, and places. Animals and inanimate objects possessed magical powers, as did some humans whom the Indians believed were witches. Ghosts, especially those of slain warriors, haunted the living until revenge had been accomplished. The sun represented a spirit or deity, called the master or preserver of breath, who was sometimes considered one with the sun. Fire represented another important being.

The Indians managed their lives well, but they realized that much of what happened in their world—illness, death, weather—was beyond their control. They had daily evidence that humans were weak and nature and the supernaturals were strong, so they performed a variety of rituals and ceremonies to appease nature, combat witchcraft, and persuade the spirit world to help them.

Indians believed they lived in an orderly universe where nature was delicately balanced and could be easily upset. They themselves upset nature when they hunted and killed animals. Therefore, they apologized to the animals ritually and purified themselves by sweating and bathing after the hunt. These actions kept nature pacified, but if they were overlooked, the animals were angered and sent disease and discomfort to humans.

Myths told by one generation to the next instructed children in the beliefs of the tribe and pointed out the dangers of neglecting the spirit world. Dreams were considered significant and were looked on as omens for the future. When things went wrong, the Indians believed the spirit world was punishing them with suffering because someone had misbehaved, either accidentally or deliberately. During these times everyone had to observe right behavior very carefully or they would pay a penalty. Sickness and death were explained as the result of broken rules and impurity. Disasters that could not be explained any other way were thought to have been the result of witchcraft.

When inexplicable things happened, the people called upon specialists to tell them what was wrong and what to do about it. There were many specialists, most of whom had something to do with curative measures to set the universe back in order. They are often referred to as conjurors, medicine men, or witch doctors, but anthropologists use the term *shaman* to refer to such practitioners. Some specialized as diagnosticians, determining the cause of the problem. Others were curers, whose job it was to correct the problem. Shamans who specialized as curers could be either men or women but were usually men. They had a broad knowledge of native herbs, learned through long apprenticeships under older shamans, as well as considerable knowledge about practical help for bruises, sprains, and broken bones. They treated people with a combination of herbs and ritual sweating and bathing.

Indians respected shamans, but they often feared them as well, for anyone who had supernatural powers might use them against other people. For this reason, shamans were often suspected of witchcraft, using the spirit world to further their own goals. Shamans were important figures, for they could help leaders persuade their people to behave. The shaman's power extended into all facets of life, and a person did not easily or comfortably defy a shaman.

Stone beads found near St. Augustine, dating from 2,000–500 B.C. They were probably acquired through trade because the stone is not native to the area.

In public ceremonies and private rituals, shamans had many duties. People called upon them not only to cure what we consider separate categories of physical and psychological ills but also to control weather, improve hunting and fishing, ensure success in war, and even make love potions. But curative ceremonies and substances would not work alone. Individuals were responsible for their own fate and were expected to behave properly, following the social rules of their community and observing fasts, taboos (forbidden practices or acts), and traditional rituals and ceremonies. If a person's behavior was not correct, no shaman could make the spirit world work on his or her behalf.

Part of the shaman's responsibility in putting nature back in balance was to determine whether anyone was polluted or had committed an act that was taboo. Many things were taboo—for instance, eating animals deemed inedible, such as snakes or bats. When a shaman determined who was at fault, he or she ordered the person to take appropriate purifying actions. In addition to sweating and bathing, purification often involved fasting. Individuals who fasted first cleaned out their stomachs with an emetic, which caused them to vomit. A drink made of herbs, called the "black drink" because of its color, was used throughout the Southeast for this purpose. After participating in acts of purification to rid themselves of pollution, individuals were once again in balance with nature

and fit to carry on their usual activities. As long as a person lived within nature's laws, all would be well.

In addition to rituals for curing and for personal purification, the Indians of the Southeast held communal feasts and festivals of thanksgiving for plentiful crops and good hunting. Throughout the year, people from the various villages of a tribe assembled for these ceremonies. However, one in particular stood out as the most significant and universally observed celebration—the Green Corn Dance.

The Green Corn Dance was a ceremony for purification, forgiveness, and thanksgiving. It took place every year at the ripening of the new crop of maize. In the far south, this occurred in the early summer; farther north, where the growing season is shorter, it was later. Although tribal differences did exist, throughout the Southeast the Green Corn Dance was very similar. The leaders of the village that would serve as host for the ceremony sent messengers to the other communities of the tribe to announce the time the dance would take place. Visitors had to arrive early in order to build temporary lodgings if the host community did not have enough housing. Because it was the responsibility of each clan to provide accommodations for its own members, clanspeople from the host village worked with visiting clan members to build shelters.

Women did not participate in the first stages of the Green Corn Dance.

Men and older boys observed a ritual fast for one or two days. Before fasting they ate a special meal of meats and vegetables from the old crops. During the fast, the men sipped the black drink, which cleared out their bodies and left them in a ritually pure state. They also discussed social problems and how to solve them.

While the men were fasting, the women cleaned their homes and extinguished the fires in their firepits to symbolize the casting out of the old and impure. They then served the men a light meal to break the fast. After the meal the men decided on forgiveness for crimes and other social transgressions short of murder. After this the head shaman of the village, who at the start of the ceremony had extinguished the fire that constantly burned in the council house, solemnly kindled a new fire, a symbol of rebirth for the community. The women took coals from this fire to start new fires at home.

After kindling the new fires, the women prepared a great feast from new crops. All of the people shared in the feast, danced, and played games. It was a joyous occasion, a combination of thanksgiving and new year's celebration with forgiveness for unacceptable behavior in the past. Young couples who had eloped, running away to avoid marriages arranged by their kin and to marry the person they preferred, returned home at the time of the Green Corn Dance and were forgiven. When this happened their elopement became an accepted marriage and they were allowed to live in the village once again.

Like the rituals performed by individuals, communal ceremonies, especially the Green Corn Dance, were thought to keep the world in order by maintaining balance, casting out impure things and ideas, and eliminating spiritual pollution. Frequent use of the black drink and fasting kept the body and mind pure and ready to start anew. After the solemn rites had been observed, these communal ceremonies were also pleasurable social events. The ceremonies united the townspeople and the neighboring communities and renewed bonds of friendship and kin.

The Green Corn Dance and other ceremonies celebrated the Indians' sacred bond with their environment. The land was their sustenance; without it their way of life would perish. The Indians, however, were not the only people to recognize the importance of the fertile Southeast. Soon Europeans would challenge them for the very wellspring of their lives. ▲

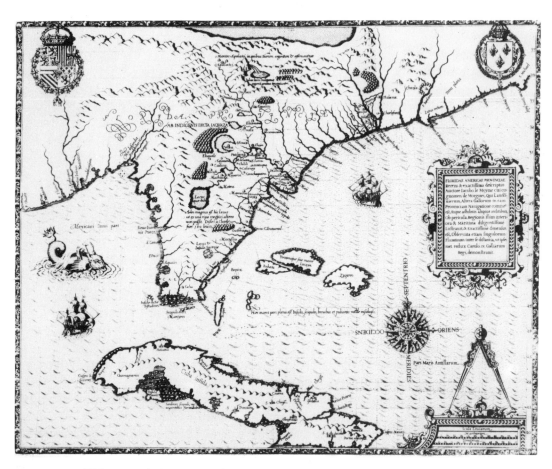

This map of Florida engraved by Theodore De Bry in 1591 was based on an earlier work by the French colonist Jacques Le Moyne.

A
TRIBE
OF
RUNAWAYS

In 1513, the Spanish explorer Juan Ponce de León sighted the land he called "Florida." Upon receiving the news of his discovery, Spain quickly claimed the territory, which extended from the southernmost tip of the Florida peninsula north to the Chesapeake Bay and west to the Mississippi River. In 1521, Ponce de León attempted to establish a settlement along the Florida coast. However, he succeeded only in antagonizing the Indians in the area, who wounded him in a skirmish. He died shortly afterward at his base in Cuba.

During the next 50 years, other Spanish explorers, among them Pánfilo de Narváez, Álvar Núñez Cabeza de Vaca, and Hernando de Soto, reinforced Spain's claim to the territory. These adventurers were not settlers, and they made little effort to take any land from the Indians. The Spanish concentrated on building forts and supply depots along the Florida coast to protect their ships from pirates as they returned to Spain and to provide a safe place to anchor when storms made the coastal waters too dangerous to travel. Although conflicts between the Spanish and the Indians over land were rare, outbreaks did occur when the Spanish "borrowed" the Indians as forced labor and as guides. The Spanish held the Indians captive, and as a result, hostilities ensued between the two.

The Indians were also subjected to a force they could not fight: disease. They had developed no immunities to the common diseases of the Europeans, so that a cold frequently turned into fatal pneumonia and smallpox destroyed whole communities. The Indians did not even have to come into face-to-face contact with Europeans; disease could be transmitted through other Indians who had picked up germs in meetings with Europeans. With no means to combat this unseen foe, the Indian population was rapidly reduced as a result of disease.

The Spanish were not the only Europeans in Florida. Huguenots (French Protestants) tried to establish a colony

Juan Ponce de León, the first Spaniard to claim Florida, called the territory Pascua Florida *(Feast of Flowers) because it was discovered at the time the Spanish held this traditional springtime celebration.*

in 1564, but the Spanish captured the settlement the following year, thus ending all French claims in Florida. During the short time the French had occupied Florida, they established good relations with the Indians. One settler, Jacques Le Moyne, sketched some of the Indians he encountered. Without his pictures and the written observations of his companion, René Goulaine de Laudonnière, little would be known about the ancient Timucua tribe that occupied northern Florida. Le Moyne's pictures are drawn in the typical style of 16th-century French artists, depicting classical gestures and body proportions,

but even so they are far more accurate and informative than any accounts by the Spanish.

In 1565, St. Augustine was founded, becoming the first Spanish and first permanent European settlement in the Southeast. The Spanish, with their superior weapons, gradually subdued Indian outbreaks against the Spanish outposts. Shortly thereafter, missionaries became active in the region and converted members of the Timucua, Calusa, and other tribes to Christianity.

Meanwhile another European nation was becoming interested in the Southeast. An English force captained by Sir Francis Drake attacked St. Augustine in 1586 but they could not penetrate the Spanish fortress. They did, however, establish a permanent settlement farther north at Jamestown, Virginia, in 1607. From then on, English interests lay in expanding their land holdings in order to grow and export crops, especially tobacco, to the mother country. England and Spain both sought to establish foreign empires, and English expansion southward inevitably worried the Spanish.

The rivalry between the two eventually involved the Indians, who sided with either the English or the Spanish. Some helped the English drive the Spanish out of what is now the state of Georgia; some even raided Spanish missions in Florida, using guns provided by their English allies to kill unarmed Florida Indians. Because Spanish policy prohibited Indians from owning guns, Indians in other parts of

The Spanish forced the Indians to work as laborers and guides. This work by the De Brys, noted Flemish engravers, shows Spaniards cruelly punishing their Indian workers.

the Southeast, as well as colonists, were easily able to capture and enslave members of the Timucua and Calusa. Many of the Florida Indians who were not killed or captured fled to the Spanish West Indies to escape their persecutors. Many others died as a result of disease. The combination of these forces led to the decline of the Indian population in Florida so that by the early 1700s the Timucua and Calusa tribes were nearly extinct.

The entire Southeast at that time was a region of massive dislocation and disorganization. The tribes living in English territory north of Florida often made war upon each other. Some of this hostility represented traditional rivalries of long standing. The English, eager to rid the area of Indians so that the land could be opened for settlement, took advantage of the discord between the tribes and frequently played one tribe off against another. As a result of this discord, many tribes were further reduced in size, and the people were often left homeless and hopeless.

As the English presence in the New World grew, colonists entered the Southeast in large numbers and settled on Indian land. In 1715, fighting broke out between the settlers and the Yamassee tribe. The Yamassee, defeated, fled into northern Florida, where the Spanish did not compete with the Indians for land. The Yamassee who resettled in Florida were granted the same rights as Spanish citizens. Soon they were joined by other displaced groups of Indians, in particular one band of Creek Indians that lived near what is now the town of Oconee, Georgia.

The territory dividing South Carolina and Florida—today the state of Georgia—served as a buffer between the colonies of Spain and Great Britain. Slavery was practiced in both colonies to satisfy the Europeans' need for farm and household laborers. Escaped African slaves, as well as Indians who had been forced into slavery, often sought refuge in this unsettled buffer region.

A 1588 map depicts Sir Francis Drake's attack on St. Augustine two years earlier.

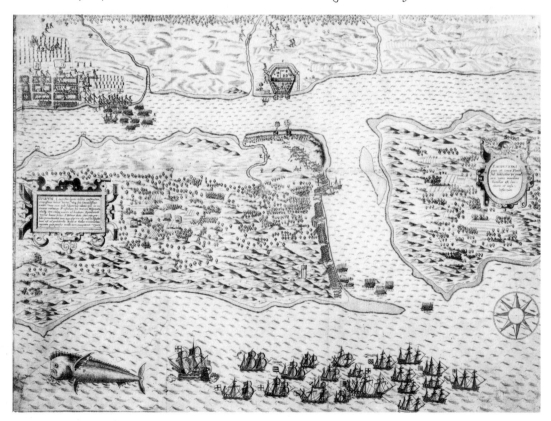

RABBIT LEARNS HOW TO BEHAVE

To entertain everyone and teach children the beliefs and customs of the tribe, Indians told stories about animals and imaginary creatures such as witches and giants. An important character found widely in Indian folklore is called an animal trickster. The trickster tried to outwit people and animals—often doing outrageous and mischievous things that were forbidden by society—and was taught a lesson in the end. Rabbit is the trickster in Seminole folklore.

Many African folktales also feature trickster animals, and it is very likely that Seminole folklore was enriched by the stories told by black fugitive slaves who joined the tribe. In the following tale, Rabbit learns how to behave.

Rabbit did not know how to behave; he bragged too much and told lies. People scolded him, and he said, "Tell me how to behave. Tell me how to do good things." So they told him to kill a rattlesnake that was frightening the people. Rabbit knew that would be very dangerous for him to do, so he thought about it for a long time. Then he sharpened a pine pole to a fine point and took it to where Rattlesnake was sitting, all coiled up. Rabbit told Rattlesnake that he had come to measure him and asked him to please uncoil so Rabbit could measure his full length. Rabbit knew that Rattlesnake would be defenseless in that position, because he could strike only from the coiled position. When Rattlesnake lay uncoiled, Rabbit took the sharp pole and killed him with it. When Rabbit brought the dead snake back, people were very impressed and told him he had done very well.

Then they told Rabbit to kill 'Gator, so Rabbit went to 'Gator's pool. When Rabbit saw the size of 'Gator, he was afraid. So he changed himself into a squirrel and climbed a tree over the pool where 'Gator lay. Squirrel said to 'Gator, "Rabbit lies all the time. He said he was going to kill you." Squirrel pretended to be a friend of 'Gator. He laughed and asked if anyone could kill 'Gator. 'Gator replied, "Rabbit does not know how, but I will tell you. A blow at the back of my head and another on my rump." Then 'Gator lay quietly in the sun. Squirrel changed back into Rabbit and hit 'Gator on the back of his head and on his rump and killed him. Then he cut off 'Gator's tail and took it back to the village. The people were amazed because they had expected Rattlesnake or 'Gator to kill Rabbit. Rabbit had fooled them all, and the people said, "You have really learned to behave."

The Spanish evacuation of Fort San Marcos in St. Augustine, which fell under British rule when Great Britain gained control of Florida in 1763.

When Great Britain established the colony of Georgia, the area was no longer a haven for runaways. Many former slaves from the British colonies then crossed the border into Florida, where they were protected by Spanish laws and given Spanish citizenship. These fugitives joined up with those Indians who had earlier fled to northern Florida to escape British oppression.

The Indians and blacks who migrated to Florida were called Seminole by the Europeans, who mispronounced the Creek word for them, *simanoli*, meaning a runaway, undomesticated, wild. Some linguists believe this word stems from the Spanish word *cimarrón*, which refers to a domesticated animal that has reverted to the wild. This term applied mostly to horses and cows, but it could also be used to describe people. Although members of this newly formed group spoke different languages, they began to favor two Muskhogean languages, Muskogee and Mikasuki. Creek Indians who were absorbed into the tribe in the 19th century would reinforce these dialects, and other tongues would be totally forgotten. (Although these languages are not mutually understandable, the Florida Seminole today still speak either Muskogee or Mikasuki.)

In 1763 Britain forced Spain to give up Florida in exchange for Cuba, which the British had captured in 1762. Shortly after the change in ownership of Florida, a British naturalist, William Bartram, visited the Seminole and noted that they had made a thoroughly satisfactory adjustment to their new lands. They were unimpeded by others in the area, because the original inhabitants, the Timucua, had become extinct as a tribe, and Europeans did not desire the land for settlement. Bartram reported that their villages were surrounded by farmland planted with oranges, corn, beans, melons, tobacco, and various squashes. He described the towns themselves as being clean, open, and airy. Bartram noted that the Seminole continued to gather wild plant foods but now purchased utensils and clothing from Europeans. Europeans also supplied the Seminole, as well as other southeastern tribes, with cloth woven from cotton and wool. Although frontier men, both Indian and European, continued to wear buckskin because of its durability, Indian women soon adopted the dress of their European counterparts: long skirts made of calico, blouses, and shawls. Gradually men would begin to reserve buckskin for use as leggings and trousers and wear cotton shirts and woolen coats and jackets.

During the short period the Seminole had lived in Florida they had forged a new identity while maintaining parts of their traditional culture. They had acquired new crops, among them melons and oranges, from the Spanish, who also introduced domesticated animals, especially horses, cows, and pigs. Many of the Seminole owned herds of cattle and became successful breeders and raisers of livestock. They continued to farm corn, squash, and beans and to hunt deer and other wild animals as they had previously done in their old tribal lands. The Seminole lived in peace with the Spanish. From time to time refugees came from the north and were absorbed into the tribe. These newcomers helped strengthen the Seminole, and a feeling of loyalty and cohesion developed among them.

In 1783, Florida again fell under Spanish dominion when Great Britain was defeated in the Revolutionary War. The new United States government forced the British to return Florida to Spain. The defeat of Britain and the subsequent formation of the United States ended the period of peace and prosperity for the Seminole. Their fertile land soon caught the attention of American settlers, some of whom trespassed onto Seminole territory and set up farms. The Indians warned these settlers that they would be attacked if they did not leave. When the Americans did not heed these warnings, the Seminole raided their homesteads.

About the same time, the owners of large plantations in the South, whose farms were worked by slaves, sought

On August 9, 1814, the Creek Indians signed the Treaty of Fort Jackson, bringing an end to the Creek War. General Andrew Jackson (seated, far right), commander of the U.S. forces involved in the fighting, negotiated the treaty that forced the Indians to give up two-thirds of their tribal lands.

ways to retrieve runaways from across the Florida border. Many of these fugitives had become members of the Seminole tribe, and the wealthy planters accused the Seminole of stealing their "property." They began to send parties of slavecatchers into Florida to recapture runaway slaves, which further incited the Seminole.

In 1812, hostilities again broke out between Great Britain and the United States. The War of 1812 aggravated animosities and rivalry among the southeastern Indians as well, some of whom sided with the United States and some of whom sided with Great Britain. In 1813, when a group of Creek Indians

captured Fort Mims, an American army post near Mobile, Alabama, and massacred the garrison, the U.S. Army retaliated. In the Creek War of 1813–14 that followed, some Creeks allied with the United States to fight against other Creeks. Many Indians died in the war, and their towns and lands were ravaged. The Indians were forced to sign a treaty with the United States, ceding all Creek lands in Georgia and some in Alabama to the federal government. Rather than live under U.S. domination, some Creeks fled to Florida, where they were incorporated into the Seminole tribe. These refugees tripled the tribe's population and strengthened its Creek characteristics.

As a result of continuing skirmishes between the Seminole and American settlers, the United States declared war on the Florida Indians in 1817. On orders from Secretary of War John C. Calhoun, U.S. troops, claiming to be on a mission to retrieve runaway slaves, entered Florida. Although this was an illegal violation of the boundary between the two nations, Spanish control in Florida was weak. Without any threat of repercussions, U.S. military raids into Spanish territory increased. Most of the Seminole's villages were burned, their livestock captured, and their food destroyed or confiscated. In addition, some of their members—both black and Indian—were taken as slaves. In the fighting, later known as the First Seminole War, American troops under General Andrew Jackson succeeded in

A woodcut showing the capture of Seminole chiefs by U.S. troops in the First Seminole War.

subduing the tribe and driving it and the Spanish southward. The Seminole, however, did not give up their land without a fight. At the Seminole village of Old Town, the Indians, led by Billy Bowlegs, faced Jackson's army, which included some Creek Indians. Although they fought fiercely, the Seminole warriors were no match for the U.S. forces, whose superior numbers and training gave them the overwhelming advantage. Many Indians were killed in the fighting, and those who survived retreated into the marshes where capture was almost impossible.

Jackson's victory in the First Seminole War led Spain to sign a treaty with the United States for the sale of Florida. On February 22, 1821, the former Spanish territory, including the Seminole's land, officially became part of the United States. Although federal control over the Seminole now passed to the United States, slaves still took refuge with the Indians, who continued to protect them. In addition, Seminole raids on United States military establishments and homesteads continued. American settlers, eager to possess the Seminole's rich farmlands but fearful of

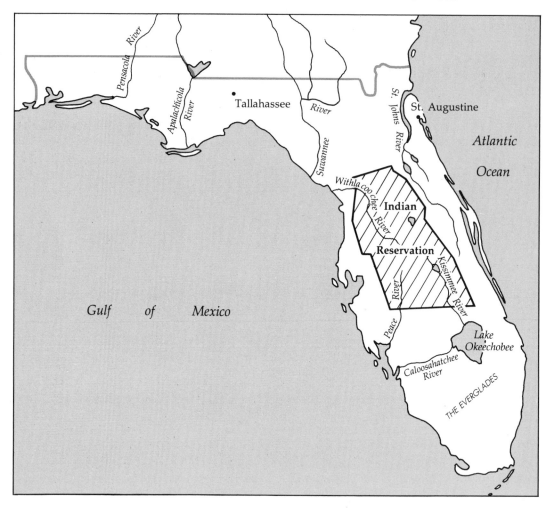

further reprisals, pushed for the removal of all Indians from Florida.

On September 6, 1823, near St. Augustine, 70 Seminole chiefs met with Florida governor William P. DuVal to discuss removal. This was the first time the United States recognized the tribe as a separate Indian nation. The U.S. government wanted to reunite the Seminole with the Creek in Georgia, but the chiefs vehemently opposed the idea.

Because of past animosities between the two tribes, the Creek were the Seminole's most hated enemy.

Instead, the Seminole agreed to move onto a reservation further south, in the center of Florida. Under the treaty signed by most, but not all, of the chiefs, non-Indians were prohibited from hunting, trespassing, or settling on the Seminole's new land. The Seminole were promised equipment, livestock, and an annual payment or annuity of $5,000 for 20 years as reparation for the loss of their land in northern Florida. The Seminole, in turn, agreed they would no longer protect escaped slaves.

In return for 30 million acres of fertile farmland, the Indians received approximately 5 million acres of land unfit for cultivation. The central Florida soil was sandy and marshy, and the area lacked the abundant game and wild plant foods that had been readily available in northern Florida.

It took the Seminole more than a year to move to the reservation. With no means to sustain themselves, the people were soon afflicted by widespread hunger. In addition, non-Indians continued to raid the Seminole's villages for runaway slaves. Although these actions blatantly violated the treaty of 1823, the Indians were too exhausted and impoverished from the recent war to resist. Many felt betrayed by the leaders who had signed the treaty. Hungry and resentful, the Seminole grew more and more discontented.

The U.S. government had carefully chosen the location of the Seminole reservation. By moving the Indians inland—away from the coast—the government effectively cut them off from access to guns and ammunition, all but crushing their chances for insurrection and collaboration with European powers unfriendly to the United States.

The Seminole soon realized that life under U.S. rule would be far different—and far less pleasant—than life under Spanish rule. As subjects of Spain, the Seminole had been given land and granted Spanish citizenship. As subjects of the United States, their land had been taken away, and they were not recognized as U.S. citizens. ▲

Osceola, the distinguished Seminole warrior and war chief, painted by George Catlin in 1837.

WAR
AND
RETREAT

The Seminole's former territory in northern Florida quickly filled with settlers eager to claim the choice agricultural and pasture land. By 1830, less than a decade after the Indians had moved to the reservation, all of the former Seminole territory had been settled and the homesteaders were clamoring for more. Pressured by these demands for additional land, the federal government planned to remove all eastern Indians, including those of Florida, west of the Mississippi River onto land acquired from France as part of the Louisiana Purchase.

The Indian Removal Act of 1830 gave President Andrew Jackson—the Indians' opponent in the First Seminole War—the authority to relocate the eastern Indian tribes. The idea of removing all Indians from the Southeast was popular with southern plantation owners and their representatives in Congress. The planters, eager to take over the Indians' traditional tribal lands, favored moving them west to new lands across

the Mississippi. The Indians would be paid an annual annuity of cash and goods for the loss of their lands.

In 1832, the Seminole became the targets of removal. The government planned to reunite the tribe with the Creeks, from whom they had broken off years earlier. If the Seminole were forced to move, they would not only lose their land and their independence but also have to live with their greatest enemy.

Some Seminole, tired of fighting and unable to see any prospect of improved conditions, agreed in principle to removal. Others, including Micanopy and King Philip (Ee-mat-la), the most important chiefs of the Seminole tribe, refused to leave. Two generations of Seminole had already faced removal from land they had settled, first from northern Florida and then from the reservation in central Florida. Each time they had rebuilt their communities and rearranged their lives. They were tired of moving only to be told to move again.

Andrew Jackson was the Seminole's foe both on the battlefield and in the presidency. He is shown here in an engraving by James B. Longacre after an 1820 painting by Thomas Sully.

The government, bent on total removal of all eastern Indians, agreed to send a few Seminole leaders to the proposed territory to evaluate it. If, upon the delegation's return to Florida, the Seminole chiefs concluded that the land was satisfactory, then—and only then—would the tribe agree to move. In late 1832, seven Seminole leaders traveled to the territory to inspect the land. While they were there they signed the Treaty of Fort Gibson, agreeing to removal, although they had no authority to act on behalf of the entire Seminole tribe.

Upon their return to Florida, the representatives claimed they had been tricked into signing the treaty through bribery, intimidation, and intoxication. The principal chiefs refused to honor the agreement, saying that the delegation was not empowered to act for the entire tribe. Nevertheless, federal officials claimed that the delegation had agreed to the land exchange and began the process of removing the Seminole from Florida.

The Seminole were given until January 1, 1836, to prepare for relocation. Some Indians began disposing of their land and livestock, but most resisted fiercely. In December 1835, one month before removal was to begin, Seminole warriors carried out a series of raids against U.S. troops stationed in Florida, triggering the long, bloody clash known as the Second Seminole War. That war, the fiercest and most expensive ever waged against American Indians, took the lives of nearly 1,500 American soldiers and uncounted Seminole and cost the U.S. government more than $20 million.

In the months following the start of the war, Seminole warriors terrorized settlers in the area, burning and pillaging the homes of wealthy plantation owners. In January 1836 alone, 16 plantations were completely destroyed by the Indians. Although the Seminole's head war chief, Osceola, resolutely opposed waiving Indian rights and yielding land, he did not participate in these raids and discouraged his warriors from doing so, saying, "It is not upon them [women and children] that we make war and draw the scalping knife; it is upon men; let us act like men."

The Seminole warriors rallied around Osceola, whose courage, leadership, and intelligence earned him the respect and confidence of his people. He taught the Indians how to use ambush and withdrawal to surprise the enemy and how to hide in wilderness that was difficult for the army to penetrate. His determination to resist removal and defend the Seminole's land inspired the other warriors and incited their fighting spirit. After one fierce battle, Osceola sent the following message to the commander of the government troops: "You have guns, and so have we; you have powder and lead, and so have we; your men will fight, and so will ours until the last drop of the Seminole's blood has moistened the dust of his hunting grounds."

In December 1836, General Thomas S. Jesup took command of the U.S. forces in Florida, which by then numbered about 10,000 soldiers. Throughout the following spring and summer, Jesup aggressively attacked the Seminole's villages, ruining their crops, cap-

Seminole warriors attack a U.S. military post in one of the many skirmishes between the Indians and government forces during the Second Seminole War (1835–1842).

(continued on page 52)

Osceola, whose courage, leadership, and intelligence helped guide the Indians in the Second Seminole War.

OSCEOLA: SEMINOLE PATRIOT AND WARRIOR

Probably the best-known Seminole—and one of the best-known American Indians—was Osceola, head war chief during the Second Seminole War.

There are no written records to confirm the details of Osceola's early life, but he is believed to have been born in 1804. His mother, a Creek of mixed ancestry, was married to a Creek man. Upon his death she married William Powell, a non-Indian of Scottish or English descent. Osceola always maintained that he was the son of his mother's first husband, but during his childhood he went by the name of Powell. At one point he claimed, "No foreign blood runs in my veins; I am a pure-blooded Muskogee." Whether or not this was true, Osceola was culturally, physically, and spiritually an Indian.

Osceola reportedly was a member of the Red Sticks, a division of the Creek tribe whose custom it was to declare war by erecting a red pole in the center of their village. After the Creek War of 1813–14, many of the defeated Red Sticks, including Osceola and his mother, moved from their traditional lands in the state of Georgia across the border to Spanish-held Florida. Like other Creeks who fled to Florida, the Red Sticks were absorbed into the Seminole tribe.

The name Osceola was apparently a corrupted English pronunciation of the warrior's war name, *Asi-yoholo* or *Assin-ye-O-La*, meaning Black Drink Singer. The name is thought to refer to the long, drawn-out cry that accompanies the ceremonial consumption of the black drink used by the Indians in rites of purification.

Osceola had two wives and several children. One wife, Chechoter (Morning Dew), was a descendant of a fugitive slave on her mother's side. Because the laws pertaining to slaveholding traced children through their mothers, Chechoter was considered a black slave and a runaway, even though her father was Indian. One day, while at a trading post with Osceola, Chechoter was captured by slavecatchers and taken to Georgia to be sold into slavery.

This was one of several incidents that led Osceola to despise non-Indians. In the fall of 1834, along with other Seminole leaders, he attended a council with the federal Indian agent General Wiley Thompson to discuss the relocation of the Indians to lands west of the Mississippi River. Osceola was ardently opposed to removal, and he advised the principal Seminole chief, Micanopy, to resist U.S. pressures for relocation. When Micanopy and several other subchiefs refused to sign the government-sponsored treaty agreeing to removal, Thompson declared that those leaders who did not sign would be struck from the roll of the Seminole chiefs and would no longer represent their tribe. Defiantly, Osceola strode to the table on which the treaty was placed and angrily declared, "The only treaty I will sign is with this!" as he plunged his knife through the document.

Osceola quickly gained recognition as a spirited, fearless leader and an eloquent speaker. As a result of his refusal to sign the removal treaty and his outspokenness against relocation, Agent Thompson had him jailed in the spring of 1835. As Osceola was led away, he vowed, "The sun is high, I will remember the hour. The agent has had his day, I will have mine."

Osceola's prophecy soon came true. After six days in prison, he was released when he appeared to have become resigned to relocation, agreeing to sign the treaty supporting removal. Nevertheless, his brief time in prison seemed only to increase his resolve to remain in Florida.

The Seminole were scheduled to begin moving west in January of 1836. At a council held in late 1835, Osceola's eloquence and encouragement convinced the Indians that they must use force to resist removal. On

Osceola angrily plunges his knife into the treaty that would make the removal of the Seminole from Florida official.

December 28, he and several warriors hid in a dense forest and ambushed Indian agent Wiley Thompson who approached with an army lieutenant. That same day, another group of warriors led by Chief Micanopy attacked a contingent of U.S. troops under Major Francis L. Dade, thus beginning the Second Seminole War.

A few days later, Osceola led the Seminole warriors in a battle against army forces commanded by General Duncan L. Clinch. Throughout the confrontation, which took place at a site along the Withlacoochee River, Osceola's shrill war cry pierced the air. As a result of the courage, skill, and leadership he demonstrated in the battle, Osceola was recognized as head war chief of the Seminole.

During the next two years, Osceola's fame spread among both Indian and non-Indian as his cunning tactics thwarted the American troops. On October 23, 1837, Osceola met with General Joseph M. Hernandez to negotiate the release of King Philip, the second chief of the Seminole, who had been captured one month earlier. The negotiations were conducted under a flag of truce. Nevertheless, Osceola and about 80 other Seminoles were captured and jailed at St. Augustine. The American public was outraged at the treacherous behavior of the U.S. Army, but their protests had little effect.

Two months later, when several Seminole warriors escaped from the St. Augustine prison, Osceola and about 200 other Seminoles who were still in jail were transferred to Fort Moultrie at Charleston, South Carolina. Shortly afterward George Catlin, the well-known painter of American Indians, visited Osceola in prison. Catlin painted several other Seminoles, but he was particularly impressed with the tribe's head war chief, whom he described as an extraordinary character and the master spirit of the tribe. Catlin said of his painting of Osceola; "I have painted him precisely in the costume in which he stood for his picture, even to a string and a trinket. He wore three ostrich feathers in his head, and a turban of a vari-colored cotton shawl—and his dress was chiefly of calicos, with a handsome bead sash or belt around his waist, and his rifle in his hand."

Osceola was ill with a high fever and a severe sore throat at the time. According to the painter, he was grieving with broken hopes and ready to die. On January 30, 1838, the day after Catlin left Fort Moultrie, Osceola died. He was buried near the fort with full military honors. His tombstone bears the inscription Patriot and Warrior.

(continued from page 47)

turing their cattle and horses, and taking their women and children hostage. These raids destroyed the Seminole's property and much of their enthusiasm for battle as well.

On October 23, 1837, near St. Augustine, Osceola and several of his warriors met with one of Jesup's officers to negotiate the release of King Philip, second chief of the Seminole tribe. King Philip had been captured earlier that fall when his village was raided by U.S. soldiers. The Indians, carrying a white flag, approached the commander, expecting him to observe the truce. The officer, however, seized the negotiation party and had them all imprisoned in St. Augustine.

Later that year a delegation of 11 Seminole chiefs, including Principal Chief Micanopy, met with General Jesup under a flag of truce to discuss a peaceful settlement to the war. These Seminole, too, were captured and imprisoned. When several of the Indians escaped, those Seminole still jailed in St. Augustine, including Osceola, were moved to a prison in Charleston, South Carolina. Soon afterward, Osceola died there. His death seemed to rekindle the Seminole's fighting spirit. King Philip's son, Cooacoochee (Wildcat), took over as head war chief. He promised to carry on Osceola's spirit of defiance, saying "I was in hopes I should be killed in battle, but a bullet would never touch me. I had rather be killed by a white man in Florida, than die in Arkansas [Territory]" (later the state of Oklahoma).

Principal Chief Micanopy was captured by the U.S. Army and imprisoned at Fort Moultrie, South Carolina, where he sat for this portrait by the artist George Catlin.

Cooacoochee continued to lead the Seminole in their fight against removal for three more years. In the spring of 1841, realizing the military might and sheer numbers of the United States forces that were against the Indians, Cooacoochee surrendered. By then, most of the Seminole, who either had given up or been captured, were relocated west of the Mississippi. With no hope of victory, the few remaining holdouts fled farther south into the Everglades.

The Second Seminole War did not end with a treaty; it merely dwindled away. The Seminole hid in the swamps, which were so difficult to penetrate that the army eventually realized military victory was impossible. Because the Indians had retreated to territory that no one else wanted, the fighting gradually ceased. On August 14, 1842, the war was officially declared over. The officer assigned to negotiate peace, Colonel Ethan Allen Hitchcock, had written about the war, "Five years ago I came [to Florida] as a volunteer, willingly making every effort in my power to be of service in punishing as I thought, the Indians. I now come, with the persuasion that the Indians have been wronged and I enter upon one of the most hopeless tasks that was ever given a man to perform." From 1835 to 1842 approximately 4,000 Seminole had been removed from Florida; the rest, who numbered around 500, remained in the swamps of southern Florida.

The environment of southern Florida was vastly different from either the Seminole's land in northern Florida or their ancestral lands in Georgia and Alabama. Southern Florida is completely flat, never more than 100 feet above sea level. Much of the ground is covered by shallow water. Only a few forested areas rise above the surrounding marsh. It was on these hummocks that the Seminole built their houses and planted their crops.

There are two seasons in southern Florida: rainy and dry. During the rainy season, from June through October, hurricanes form and sometimes do serious damage. During the dry season, from November through May, there are occasional droughts.

Around and north of Lake Okeechobee, the land is somewhat higher and better drained. Although the soil is sandy, the topsoil is fairly rich and can be cultivated for a period. However, the soil is quickly depleted, and the cultivator must frequently clear new ground. Several varieties of pine trees are native to the northern Everglades and in the swamps cypress trees grow Palmetto palms are common throughout.

Cypress trees rise out of the swamps of southern Florida.

Because they could no longer grow much of their food or maintain herds of cattle, the Seminole became gatherers, making use of the many kinds of wild plants available. The area has an abundance of game, so the Seminole could continue to hunt deer, bear, otter, raccoon, squirrel, and rabbit. They also hunted some species of birds, more for their feathers than for food, although they did eat some, such as ducks and turkeys. Turtles and alligators could also be found, as well as a wide variety of fresh- and salt-water fish. The deadly water moccasin or cottonmouth lived in many of the swampy areas, and the rattlesnake could be found in the drier areas. The Seminole, however, did not eat snakes.

For the next decade, the Seminole were largely left alone. The non-Indians in Florida seemed almost to have forgotten them. In 1855, however, surveyors sent to map the Everglades pillaged the garden of the Seminole chief, Billy Bowlegs. They took the ripe produce and destroyed the rest of the crops. The Indians retaliated and wounded several of the survey party. During the next three years similar skirmishes occurred as U.S. soldiers renewed the drive to remove all Seminole from Florida. In 1858, Billy Bowlegs—the last chief under whom all the Florida Seminole were united—and 162 of his people agreed to move west of the Mississippi River.

Only a few Seminole still remained in Florida. They retreated farther into the swamps, where it was almost impossible for the government to pressure them into leaving. The terrain was too difficult for government troops to mount an attack. Even if the army had gotten through and destroyed their small gardens, the Indians would still have enough food for survival because the Everglades were blessed with ample game, fish, and wild plant foods. The offer of money in exchange for relocation had little appeal for most Seminole. A few accepted the bribes, but most merely ignored them and remained out of reach in the swamps.

The federal government continued trying to persuade the fugitives to move west until the Civil War, when it became too busy with that conflict to bother with the Seminole question. From 1861 until the end of the century the Seminole of Florida were largely disregarded, because the land they occupied was not considered desirable by non-Indian settlers.

Although the government paid little attention to the Seminole in the last part of the 19th century, the Indians were not completely isolated from the outside world. By the 1880s they were selling hides and some produce and crafts to non-Indians in exchange for the trade goods they had become accustomed to: cloth, rifles and ammunition, metal items, tobacco, and some foods such as coffee and tea. Sometimes a journalist visited to write about the tribe.

In 1880, the newly organized Bureau of American Ethnology, a branch of the Smithsonian Institution, sent an investigator, Clay MacCauley, to survey the Seminole. He wrote an account of his observations in the bureau's *Fifth Annual Report*. MacCauley located five small Seminole communities living in southern Florida with a total population of only 208 people. (Although there are no reliable census data, it is highly likely that MacCauley did not reach all of the Seminole's settlements and that his figure is a bit low; the population was probably less than 500.) These communities had no overall tribal organization or civil government to enact rules or laws. MacCauley noted that each community contained several camps or residences of extended families related through women—the traditional matrilocal society of the southeastern Indians—and each camp was composed of individual households of Indians living together as an extended family. Camps were the basic unit of Seminole life in southern Florida; people referred to themselves as belonging to a camp or to a family.

A typical camp household contained several structures, each used for a different purpose: sleeping, dining, relaxing. The Seminole adapted their traditional houses to the semitropical climate and weather conditions of southern Florida. The buildings, called *chickees* (prounounced with the accent on the last syllable: chic-KEE) by the Mikasuki-speaking Seminole, were open-sided to let cooling breezes through and had a thatched roof made of palmetto fronds. Each chickee was built on a platform of split palmetto logs

A Seminole chickee, in a drawing from Clay MacCauley's account in the Fifth Annual Report *of the Bureau of American Ethnology, 1887.*

A Seminole family wearing the typical clothing of the Florida Indians in the late 1800s.

that was raised about 30 inches off the ground to protect the people and their belongings from the mud and rain. Chickees were the typical summer house of the southeastern Indians adapted to local materials and conditions.

The camp usually had a cookhouse, which protected the fire used for food preparation from the frequent rains. The cookhouse was a small structure with a thatched roof that was supported by tree trunks. Smoke filtered easily through the thatch, although it blackened the rafters, as well as the pots and other utensils that hung from the beams, with soot. The floor of the cookhouse was made of packed dirt. The fire, constructed on a raised earthen hearth to prevent it from being extinguished during high water, was fed by a circle of logs that radiated from the center of the ashes like spokes on a wheel. As the fire consumed the end of a log, the unburned portion was pushed closer to the center.

Within each community the people visited among camps. Visiting between communities occurred less frequently because of the great distances from one settlement to another. Hospitality was always important to the Seminole. Visitors expected to join in meals, and hosts enjoyed having guests and learning the latest news. There was usually a pot of stew simmering on the fire so that food was ready whenever a family member or visitor became hungry. Likewise, a pot of coffee usually sat warming in the fire's ashes.

Life in a Seminole camp was not regulated by clocks. The people rose with the sun and ate a morning meal. Then each person went about the day's tasks. Women usually stayed in the camp, caring for children, preparing food, and making clothing. Occasionally they worked on nearby plantations, planting and picking produce for wages, but usually they farmed only their own garden plots.

Depending on the season and family need, men hunted, fished, or hired out as agricultural laborers when there was work. Sometimes, if there were no jobs available, they lounged around the camp. In the evening, they joined the women, children, and any guests at mealtime. The food they ate was a version of the traditional southeastern diet, adapted to regional plants and animals: meat, fish, or turtle stew; frybread; coffee; and *sofki,* the southeastern Indian's traditional drink of boiled corn. Tropical fruits often accompanied the meal. Eating was a time for relaxation and socializing. Everyone, especially the children, looked forward to the storytelling that would follow.

There was no school for the children to attend. They learned as they grew by watching their parents and others as they worked. As the occasion allowed, adults gave the children small tasks to perform that were within their ability. Girls learned to cook, sew, and tend babies by helping their mothers and aunts. Boys accompanied their fathers and uncles on hunting and fishing trips. There was little pressure to perform or to compete. Each child grew to competence without grades or restrictions. Young Seminole knew that someday they would be responsible for maintaining and feeding the family and camp, and they accepted that responsibility.

Toward the turn of the century the hand-cranked sewing machine became a common appliance in the camp, and women began to elaborate on the traditional calico dresses and shirts the Indians wore. They sewed bands of cloth in contrasting colors and designs onto the clothing. The women worked independently but in groups, enjoying the small talk and gossip that their company offered. Over their dresses Seminole women wore a short cape around their shoulders. They draped strings of beads around their necks and added to them through the years so that by old age a woman might have accumulated so many necklaces that they formed a solid band extending from her shoulders to her chin. Men's clothing had changed over time from garments made of leather to long calico shirts (kilts), and cotton turbans. Like the women, the men wore beaded necklaces, although they wore only several strings at a time.

The camp centered on the extended family was a focal point of Seminole life. The traditional matrilocal society endured through many moves and troubles, and it acted as a stabilizing influence, giving psychological security to people who had suffered hardship for nearly a century. The sense of belonging to a family and camp maintained Seminole identity when no overall tribal leadership existed. ▲

The introduction of the sewing machine led to a change in the style of clothing worn by the south Florida Indians. A distinctly Seminole fashion evolved, with garments featuring bands of colorful patchwork.

4

MAKING
A
NEW LIFE

As the 20th century began, the Seminole people in southern Florida were living in small groups scattered through otherwise unoccupied territory in the interior of the peninsula. This region of swamps and saw grass (a plant with leaves that have sharp edges) began about 65 miles north of Lake Okeechobee and extended southward to just below the city of Miami. Within these boundaries, Seminole settlements were located as far west as the present town of Immokalee and as far east as the present town of Davie. This territory was almost the same as that occupied by the extinct Calusa.

On the coasts directly east and west of the Seminole area, non-Indian settlements were springing up with the help of money from northern developers. For the most part, the Indians were ignored by the dominant society that was beginning to flourish on the coasts. The only contact the Seminole had with non-Indians was with occasional traders. Those who lived in camps closest to Miami did more business with outsiders than any of the other settlements. Contacts with traders, infrequent though they were, supplied manufactured items that the Indians were eager to obtain. But an increased desire for trade goods would soon force more frequent and longer interactions with the outside world.

Left to themselves and no longer oppressed by military action or the threat of further removal, the Seminole still faced two challenges. An immediate problem was finding ways to make a living in southern Florida. In addition, they were trying to maintain some tribal unity among many widely dispersed communities. This was especially difficult because the Indians were divided into two linguistic groups—Muskogee and Mikasuki.

Indians from the various Seminole groups did travel to see each other. Because the distances were fairly great between them, sometimes more than 100 miles, visitors usually stayed for extended periods, even several months. These prolonged visits enabled the Indians to maintain a network of communication. Sometimes they resulted in marriages, which strengthened ties between the various communities.

Had they been forced to, the Seminole could have been totally self-sufficient. They had learned how to grow most of their own foodstuffs on the high land—the hummocks—in the swamps. They also were able to raise pigs, chickens, and a few head of cattle. To supplement the food they obtained from these sources, they hunted. However, by the beginning of the 20th century the Seminole had become dependent on manufactured goods. Containers made of metal had replaced pottery and basketry, and guns had long since replaced bows and arrows. These items, as well as coffee, tobacco, and cloth, were no longer just luxury items; they were necessities. In addition, the Seminole had adopted the currency of the United States as their medium of exchange. They most commonly used the quarter, not the dollar, because most items cost much less than a dollar. When trading with outsiders, the Seminole would either ask for currency in exchange for goods or accept credit, which was recorded in the form of marks on paper, one mark for each quarter owed.

In the first part of the 20th century, almost no Seminole were able to work for regular wages. Some found part-time or seasonal work on farms or ranches, but there were very few jobs to be found in the area where the Seminole lived. The answer to their cash problems lay in an unexpected direction: women's fashion. For several decades, the Seminole were able to provide an abundant supply of feathers, otter pelts, and especially alligator hides, all of which were greatly prized by designers and manufacturers of clothing.

During the last part of the 19th century and well into the 20th century, American women wore large hats lavishly trimmed with feathers. Among the most highly prized feathers were those of various species of heron, which flourished in the south Florida swamps. In their mating season, the male herons are adorned with brightly colored crests of feathers. The Indians could make an easy profit by catching the birds and selling their plumage to traders, who in turn marketed them to people in the fashion industry.

In a similar way, the Seminole capitalized on the demand for alligator handbags, shoes, and other accessories. Alligators ranged all through Florida and were particularly plentiful in the rivers and swampy lowlands of southern Florida. Adult alligators are large, sometimes reaching a length of 19 feet. Consequently, they are dangerous, with rows of sharp teeth and powerful jaws and tail. Now that the Seminole had rifles, they could easily kill the animals from a distance. The hides were valuable for trade, but the meat was also prized by the Seminole, who especially liked the taste of young, tender alligators.

Otter pelts were used to trim women's clothing or were made into coats, muffs, and tippets, garments similar to stoles or scarves. As they did with the feathers and hides, the Indians traded the pelts either for goods or for cash. With the demand for plumage and skins, it took only a few hunters in each camp to bring in sufficient trade goods or money to satisfy Seminole needs. Because there was little competition from outsiders for their hunting grounds, all these natural resources were in plentiful supply at the time.

In the early years of the 20th century, the Florida state government began planning changes that would open the area to settlement and develop the state economically. One plan endorsed by the state legislature in 1905 was to drain the swampy Everglades to bring drinking water to the east coast cities and create land useful for large-scale agriculture. A system of canals was devised to channel the ground water away. Both the change in the flow of water and the creation of the canal network had injurious environmental impacts on the wildlife of the area. Eventually these changes would affect the Indians as well.

In addition, the state began a program to develop its transportation system. Railway lines were constructed along the east coast to improve access to southern Florida. This led to a rapid

A barge with machinery brought in to drain the Everglades in 1921. The state of Florida undertook the drainage project in the early 20th century to bring drinking water to the coastal cities and create land suited to large-scale agriculture.

increase in the coastal population. As the coastal area filled up, ranchers and farmers moved into the interior of the state to find the acreage they needed. They began clearing and fencing land for pastures and fruit groves. The Seminole, who had been camping and hunting at will there, were now cut off from much of this land.

Land conflicts would continue into the 1920s. During that decade there was a land boom in Florida real estate. Settlers, homeowners, and developers joined the farmers and ranchers in the interior. They created communities that grew from small settlements into cities.

The building of railroads, highways, and houses in southern Florida in the 1920s led to a land boom. This cartoon appeared in the November 26, 1925, issue of Life *magazine.*

The state began an extensive highway building program, and the east coast soon became a resort for wealthy people from the northeastern part of the United States. All of this meant that the Seminole now had less land over which to roam.

The Bureau of Indian Affairs (BIA) became aware of the land problems of the Seminole as Floridians tried to enclose lands to avoid contact with the Indians. The bureau tried to help the Indians. In 1911 federal legislation created two reservations in Florida, Big Cypress Reservation and Dania Reservation, where the Indians would be protected from encroachment on their land. Big Cypress Reservation is in the center of the peninsula, about 30 miles south of the town of Clewiston, which is near Lake Okeechobee. It comprises 42,880 acres. Dania Reservation, which is now called Hollywood Reservation, has only 480 acres and is near the east coast of Florida, west of the city of Hollywood. In 1926 it became the site of the BIA's agency for the tribe. A federal superintendent or agent appointed by the bureau heads the agency.

Some Seminole accepted the reservations as a new place to live. The first Indians to move onto the reservations built their traditional thatch-roofed housing. Like their ancestors, they built

WHERE TWO WORLDS MEET

As a result of their contact with missionaries and other non-Indians for several centuries, the Seminole's deepest beliefs have become thoroughly permeated by Christian ideology. Their traditional mythology has been almost completely lost. Traces of original myths remain, however, in stories such as the following one about the creation of humanity. This origin myth was told by an aged shaman who was not a Christian convert. He believed the tale he told was authentically Seminole.

Fishakikomechi, the Creator, made the world. Before that there was just water. Then he put animals and plants on the earth and made a man he called Adam. Adam was the only person and he got lonely. So the Creator made a woman and called her Eve. There was a plant that they could not eat, but a snake told them it was all right to eat it. Eve gave it to the man, and he ate it, and then they knew they were naked, so they hid. They made clothes from leaves, and eventually they had children of all different colors. That is why there are so many different people in the world.

But later there was too much drinking and too many wives, so Noah built a boat and took animals and people away with him. Water came over the land and the other people were drowned. The people on the boat went back to the land when the water went down and had lots of children.

Jesus came and preached to them, but some people hated him and killed him. He arose and went to his followers and they had a feast with wine. Jesus said that since people had killed him, he was not going to live on the earth anymore, but first he taught people how to grow corn, and that is how the people came to have corn.

The narrator of this myth, a Seminole shaman (left), with his wife outside their home.

family camps of several chickees, one for sleeping and others for food preparation and socializing. To protect their bedding and belongings from wind-driven rains, they suspended canvas sheets from the eaves. The sheets could be rolled up or lowered as weather conditions required. In this way they preserved the traditional chickee style, with modifications.

The Seminole did not participate in World War I (1914–18), but ultimately they were affected by it. The demand for feathers and hides in the international fashion trade slumped during the war. Finally it collapsed completely. To compensate for the loss of that market, the Indians engaged in other activities. Women began to make dolls for sale to non-Indians. They constructed the dolls from native materials such as palmetto fiber and dressed them in Seminole clothing. A few men earned cash by working as guides for non-Indian hunters during the hunting season. Some Indians continued to find seasonal work as agricultural laborers.

Although reservation land had been authorized for the Seminole, they were slow to move onto it. They still lived in scattered, often isolated camps. Because of their long history of forced removal, they were suspicious of efforts to move them onto reservation land. They also had made reasonably good adjustments to the south Florida land where they were living. Other families and individuals had learned that being

Tourists stroll along the sand at Palm Beach, one of the popular resort areas that sprang up in southern Florida in the early 1900s.

(continued on page 73)

PATCHES OF COLOR

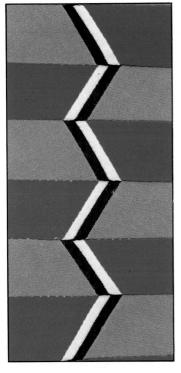

A close-up of a Seminole patchwork strip. Many small patches are stitched together to form a strip long enough to band a skirt.

When the Seminole acquired hand-cranked sewing machines from non-Indian traders in the late 1800s, their style of clothing changed. The women began to sew bands or strips of contrasting colored cloth onto the calico skirts and shirts they made. Eventually the stitched decorations became more elaborate: The women pieced together scraps of material in patchwork designs to produce the colorful bands. Seminole women continue to create this intricate stitchery today. Some of the designs are traditional and have been used for many years. Sometimes a traditional pattern is altered by a sewer to suit her individual tastes. Many patterns have names, often based on the item that they resemble, such as arrows or spools. The most complex designs may be elaborations on one traditional pattern or combinations of two or more simpler patterns. These complex designs are sometimes known by the name of the woman who created the pattern.

Since the 1940s Seminole women have alternated rows of rickrack or ribbon trims with bands of patchwork on the garments they sew. Designs differ between the reservations: At Big Cypress, the women generally use six or seven bands of smaller designs, whereas at Brighton the women use one wide band. Both styles are found at Brighton and Big Cypress, however, because designs are often admired and copied widely by other women. Copying a design is considered to be an honor to its creator, who does not feel that she has an exclusive claim to her pattern.

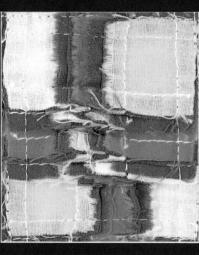

A patch in the checkers pattern resembles some variations of the traditional nine-patch used in American quilts. The wrong side of the patch shows how the cloth pieces are fitted and stitched together.

Some patchwork designs have been used by Seminole women on all the reservations for many years. Sewers often modify traditional patterns. At left is one variation of the checkers design.

The right and wrong sides of the patchwork design known as arrows.

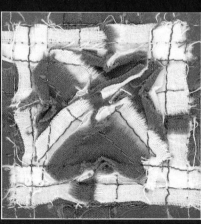

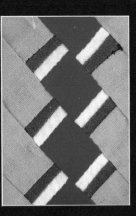

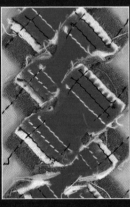

Traditional designs are often named for objects they resemble. This design, which looks like spools of thread leaning against one another, is known as spools.

A variation of the checkers design.

The creator of this design called it "flash" because it reminded her of the bolt of lightning emblazoned on the chest of the comic-strip character Flash.

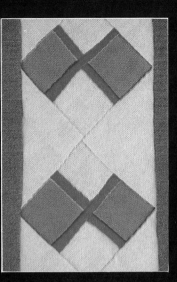

The right and wrong sides of a strip containing the design known as Xs.

A close-up of one patch in the rattlesnake design. A row of these patches sewn in a continuous strip resembles the diamondback rattler.

The right and wrong sides of a strip of patches in another version of the checkers pattern.

A man's shirt typical of the style worn by the Seminole in the early 1900s.

A woman's skirt and cape dating from the 1940s. The sewer combined thin bands of ribbon trim with wider strips of patchwork.

(continued from page 64)

a tourist attraction had cash value, and they were reluctant to leave the source of their income and move to reservations.

Tourism, which a half-century later would become the leading industry of the state, was in an early stage of development in the beginning of the 1900s. As popular winter resorts began springing up along the Atlantic and Gulf coasts and hard-surfaced roads were built through the interior of the peninsula, a few Seminole started visiting the tourist centers in the winter. Resort owners encouraged them to stay and build their traditional open-sided thatch-roofed dwellings and create small villages. The villages would serve as exhibits for curious tourists and show the daily life of the people, their housing, and their customs. Some Indians enjoyed this and found it to be an alternative way to make a living. The pay, about $6.00 per family per week, was good for that time. Other Seminole, however, thought such display was demeaning and believed they should remain isolated from all but the most necessary non-Indian contact.

At some of the tourist centers, Seminole men began the practice of wrestling alligators. Tourists would pay to see the sport and often leave generous tips with the wrestler. Many people think that alligator wrestling is a traditional sport of the Seminole because of the publicity given to it, but this is not the case. It is an exceedingly dangerous activity; several men have been maimed for life while wrestling alligators. The sport continued only because of the good money that the Indians could make from it.

Along with the rest of the nation, the Seminole suffered during the Great Depression of the 1930s. The U.S. economy stagnated during the depression, and millions of people were unemployed. As yet, few Indians had moved onto the federal reservations. Most were largely self-sufficient, surviving by living off the land—hunting, fishing, and cultivating small plots on their hummocks. What the Indians did lack were the manufactured items that they had come to desire.

To pay for these, they sought wage labor and took jobs as agricultural workers wherever they could find them. Some joined migratory farm laborers who worked the fields of the state, moving as crops ripened. Often, whole families moved to accompany the prime wage earner. Occasionally a hunter could still sell game or hides, but that market supplied very little income because demand for them was low. Women visited relatives in tourist centers, bringing handcrafts to sell, but there was little tourism in the 1930s.

In their efforts to find work for wages, the Seminole had increasingly frequent contact with non-Indians. They sometimes lived on farms while working as agricultural laborers. These increased contacts brought greater knowledge of and interest in the outside world. As they came to understand the ways of non-Indian society, the Seminole's fear of outsiders lessened.

Missionaries, especially from the Episcopalian and Baptist faiths, were another source of interaction between the Seminole and the non-Indian society. These people first set out to make friends with the Seminole, but wherever possible they also attempted to convert the Indians to Christianity. Through the missionaries, the Seminole learned more about the outside world. Until the 1940s, the missionaries did not convert many Indians, but in time the conversion of a few respected individuals prompted others to follow their example. Josie Billie was an important shaman who became a convert. It was not an easy decision for him because conversion meant the loss of much that the Seminole held dear. He did continue some ritual practices, even though he abandoned his sacred medicine bag.

In an effort both to encourage the Seminole to move onto reservation lands and to provide them with a more stable source of income, the government developed work programs at the Dania Reservation. The programs came under the public works and job training program of the Civilian Conservation Corps (CCC), one of the government agencies that had been created as part of President Roosevelt's New Deal. Under CCC programs, workers would receive on-the-job training, along with food, housing, and a cash stipend, while they did useful work. The CCC project for the Seminole, which provided medical assistance as well as other benefits, had them clear reservation land of timber so that the Indians' farm plots could be enlarged. There were plenty of pine trees to cut down, and large areas of land also had to be cleared of timber that had fallen during a severe hurricane in 1926. In the process of clearing land, some men learned how to operate heavy trucks and machinery. In the 1930s under state and federal relief programs some Indians also found employment on the road crews that improved the state highway system. These jobs taught them other skills, such as how to grade and pave roads.

In 1935 the federal government created a third reservation for the Seminole, Brighton Reservation, on the northwestern shore of Lake Okeechobee. The state of Florida also designated 108,000 acres of land at the southeastern portion of Big Cypress Reservation as a state reservation. Today this state land is still used only for hunting.

There was little change on the reservations during the 1940s. Very few Seminole served in the military in World War II (1941–45), and the war had little impact on them. There were some possibilities for war-industry employment in Florida, but none of these jobs were on or near the reservations. For the most part, the Seminole did not have the skills required for defense jobs. Most had little or no schooling and were only qualified for unskilled jobs in defense industries, and few Seminole held even these.

There had been no provision for formal education for the Seminole until after World War I. An elementary school was established at Dania Reservation in 1927 but was closed in 1936 when officials decided to encourage children to attend public schools off the reservation. The officials believed that the young Indians would benefit from increased interaction with children from the general population.

In the 1930s and 1940s, a few Seminole children were sent to Indian boarding schools. These boarding schools were far away, in distant states, and the prolonged separation from their families was very hard on the children. With no friends or family close by, they suffered from feelings of homesickness. The schools, established in the late 1800s to teach the Indians how to be good U.S. citizens and deemphasize their Indian heritage, made the students feel strange and inadequate. More successful and pleasant for the young Seminole were schools on the reservations or in nearby communities. In the 1940s the first Seminole student was awarded a high school diploma.

More people moved onto the reservations in the 1940s, partly as a result of encouragement by federal officials but more significantly because of the example set when a few respected individuals moved onto them. On the reservations, the Seminole continued to build their traditional dwellings. By this time some Seminole had learned to drive and enjoyed the experience and convenience of having a car. A few families built shelters for the cars they owned. They could afford only used models, often in poor condition, but the people learned enough about auto mechanics to keep them running.

One reservation was settled somewhat differently from the rest. In 1926 Dania Reservation was established as a center for Seminole who were sick or unable to adjust to their new environment. That year the federal government built 10 cottages and an administration building on the reservation. The following year a school and other buildings were added. Not until after World War II did this reservation become more populated with other Seminole who built their own homes.

By the middle of the 20th century, the Seminole had fully adjusted to their environment and were making a comfortable living in southern Florida. However, maintaining a sense of tribal unity was still a problem. For one thing, Mikasuki speakers lived at Big Cypress, Muskogee speakers lived at Brighton, and speakers of both languages lived at Dania. In addition, many Indians were still living in isolated groups, and the people were unorganized as a tribe. Not until the second half of the century would the Seminole more directly address the problem of maintaining their unity. ▲

Throughout years of relocation and separation, the Seminole's tradition of establishing new families near the wife's mother's family helped maintain stability.

THE
FORMATION
OF THE
TRIBE

In the 1950s the Seminole made a general migration onto reservation lands. The move followed the sporadic shift that took place during the 1940s. There were several reasons for the upswing in reservation population: Many influential and respected elders led the way; federal agents were persuasive in their argument for the advantages of reservation life; commercial farms, orchards, and ranches expanded, taking over land that the Seminole had freely moved over; and, finally, as Florida's general population grew, more and more land was developed for residential and commercial purposes. In the 1950s, the population of Florida grew faster than anywhere else in the United States. It had become almost impossible for the Seminole to continue their seasonal migrations through territory that was becoming increasingly fenced in.

By the mid-1950s, most Seminole lived for at least part of the year on one of the reservations. The rest of the year they worked on fruit and vegetable farms, usually living in housing provided by the farm owners. The only significant population of Seminole living on off-reservation land was located along U.S. Route 41, the highway from Miami to Tampa. The road had been carved in 1928 through the heart of the Everglades and followed the old Indian route, Tamiami Trail. The families who lived on public or private lands along this way were called the Tamiami Indians or Trail Indians. They were considered "squatters" because they did not have rights to the land or pay rent to live on it. The dozen or so families living along the trail represented the most culturally conservative of all the Seminole. They continued their traditional practices and were the least interested in adopting non-Indian ways.

Although the Indians were settling together on the three reservations, there was no tribal government to make regulations or to represent the Seminole in dealing with non-Indians. A loosely organized council composed of repre-

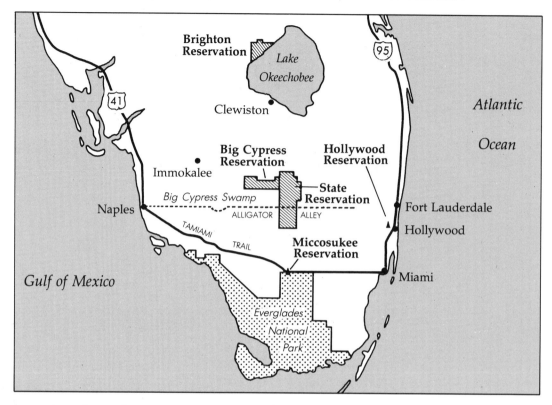

sentatives from the various communities had met occasionally in the early years of the 20th century, but it did not have the power to enforce any of its decisions. There was no one person regarded as chief or leader by all the Seminole. The last person to have been recognized as chief was Billy Bowlegs, a century earlier.

With no tribal council or other representative body, the Seminole felt that they had no one who could speak on their behalf to the local governments. Consequently, they never participated in elections or the selection of officials. Their chief official was the federal superintendent who was "given" or as-

signed to them by the BIA; they had nothing to say about the appointment.

In 1934, however, the federal government had created a mechanism by which Indian groups could incorporate and form a political organization with elected officials. This legislation was the Indian Reorganization Act (IRA). In August 1957, some of the Seminole used this act to draw up a constitution and organized themselves as the "Seminole Tribe of Florida." The Seminole Tribe of Florida continues to be governed by this constitution today.

The government of the Seminole Tribe of Florida has two parts, a council and a board of directors. Adult members of the Tribe elect representatives for each of the three federal reservations to the council and the board. Each reservation is represented by one council member and one board member. Only residents of a reservation are allowed to vote for its representatives, but members from all the reservations elect the chairperson of the council and the president of the board. Anyone 21 years or older may be a candidate for the council or the board, provided the person is a member of the Tribe and has lived continuously on one of the reservations for four years. Several women have held positions on the council and the board, and in 1967 Betty Mae Jumper became the first woman to be elected chairperson.

The primary responsibilities of the council are to negotiate with state, federal, and local agencies and to formulate and enforce laws. The board takes care of business matters for the Tribe and is responsible for developing and managing tribal resources. Both bodies meet at Hollywood Reservation (formerly called Dania Reservation), which was designated Tribal Headquarters in 1957.

An early photograph of U.S. Route 41, the old Tamiami Trail, along which some of the Seminole Indians lived.

Betty Mae Jumper, the first woman to be elected chairperson of the council of the Seminole Tribe of Florida.

Indians must apply to the council for membership in the Seminole Tribe of Florida. The most important prerequisite for membership is that they be one-quarter or more Seminole by birth—that is, they must have at least one fully Seminole grandparent, or two who were half-Seminole. Majority approval by the council is required for acceptance. Members may live on reservations or on nonreservation lands in rural areas or in towns or cities, but only members on the reservations are eligible to vote for their representatives to the council or the board.

The Seminole Tribe of Florida is the largest organized group of Indians in the state. However, some Florida Indians do not belong to it. They may be of other tribes, or they may be Seminole who have not formally joined, even though they may live on one of the reservations. Indians who are not members of the Seminole Tribe of Florida are not eligible to vote on tribal matters.

The Tamiami Indians did not join with the other Seminole to organize the Seminole Tribe of Florida and its council and board. They remained aloof from any formal political organization until 1962. Then they too used the Indian Reorganization Act to set up their own structure. They named themselves the Miccosukee Tribe. This smaller tribe has its headquarters on trust land that was specifically set aside by the federal government for the Indians' use. This land is about 40 miles west of Miami, at a point on U.S. Route 41 that is sometimes called 40-Mile Bend. Most of the Miccosukee Tribe live there, but other Miccosukee also live on nonreservation land in small campsites along the Tamiami Trail, where they hunt, fish, and sell souvenirs to tourists. However, these Miccosukee are squatters on land not their own, and it is likely that they will some day have to move elsewhere. The Miccosukee who live on trust land along the northern boundary of the Everglades National Park sometimes work as park guides, taking tourists on airboats, which are specially designed to move through the shallow wetlands. They also have a restaurant on the federal land and an arts and crafts store.

Although they have organized separately, the Miccosukee Indians are descended from the same earlier

Billy Cypress, being sworn in as chairman of the Miccosukee Tribe in 1987.

populations as the members of the Seminole Tribe of Florida, and there are many links of kinship between the two groups. Because they are descended from the same people, Miccosukee Tribe members have the same rights as members of the Seminole Tribe of Florida to fish and hunt on the state reservation land that borders Big Cypress Reservation to the southeast.

Descendants of the Seminole who relocated to land west of the Mississippi continue to live in Oklahoma. These Seminole, however, are not a recognized tribe, and they have retained little of the traditional Seminole culture.

The development of their political system was the most dynamic and far-reaching event of the 20th century for the Seminole. The ability to make and enforce decisions on the reservations and to discuss plans and problems common to all became a source of pride. The Seminole began to vote on issues pertaining to them, such as developing tribal resources. Today they consider public discussion as important as any other U.S. citizen does. Learning to debate and vote on local issues prepared many to feel comfortable enough to make decisions and vote in state and national elections.

After the formal creation of the Seminole Tribe of Florida, tribal officials decided to develop resources on the reservations to provide income for the Tribe. One plan they agreed on was to lease some of their tribal land to large commercial vegetable growers. These companies would cultivate the land, improving it with drainage systems and fertilizer over a period of three to six years, depending on their contract. Then they would return the land to the Tribe. All of this activity would be supervised by the federal government. Under this plan the Tribe would end up with fertile land where there once had been swamp.

The plan succeeded. In addition to improved, drained fields, the Seminole also gained upgraded roads into their reservations because the growers needed easy access to the fields. Eventually a major east-west highway was built that crossed the southern portion of the state reservation. From this toll-road, called Alligator Alley, an access road was built to Big Cypress Reservation.

The hard-surfaced roads brought about much greater contact between the Indians and the non-Indian world. They not only traveled to the small towns close to the reservations but also visited larger coastal cities such as Fort Lauderdale and Miami. This incentive for travel has been more important for residents of Big Cypress and Brighton than for those at Hollywood because these reservations are geographically isolated.

Gradually, traditional hunting of such animals as deer and alligator and cultivation of small gardens has been replaced by an economy based almost totally on money. Food and other necessities are purchased at stores in town. In 1967 and 1968 the Tribe operated its own store on Big Cypress Reservation. Although this enterprise brought income to the Tribe, the store had to be closed because of problems with staffing and vandalism.

Another source of income for the Tribe was more successful. When the improved fields were returned to the Seminole by the commercial growers, they were not turned into large tribal farmlands or plantations. Beginning in 1960, they were turned into pastures planted with grasses superior to the grasslands native to Florida. With the help of federal government loans, the Tribe established cattle herds. Many Seminole men, as well as a few women, entered into stock raising as an industry. The cattle industry flourished at Big Cypress and Brighton, which had sufficient acreage, and Seminole from Hollywood could own and pasture their cattle at either of these areas. Earlier efforts to raise cattle at both Big Cypress and Brighton had been unprofitable because of the poor quality of the grass, resulting in poor grades of beef and low production of calves. Not until the native grasses had been replaced could truly successful stockbreeding become a possibility. The improved pastures also meant that better breeds of cattle, such as Angus, could be raised.

Herding cattle at Brighton Reservation, 1950. The Seminole had been raising cattle since the Spanish introduced domesticated animals more than two centuries earlier.

The cattle program affected the Seminole in various ways, not just from an economic standpoint. Those who owned successful herds benefited as their yearly income increased. They also expanded their understanding of animal husbandry and marketing as professional agronomists from the state taught the Seminole how to raise and sell healthy cattle. This new knowledge, coupled with their considerable investment in the project, led to greater participation in decision making on the reservations. They became more interested in politics and tribal elections because they wanted representatives who understood and supported their positions. Cattle owners themselves tended to be candidates for office more frequently than did other Seminoles.

Some Indians who tried to become cattle raisers failed, however. They then became hostile to the others, making angry comments and gossiping about those who were successful. These Seminole thought the successful cattle owners were secretly collaborating with the Seminole agency, and they refused to participate in making community decisions. They felt they had been denied a share in the benefits of the cattle-industry program. The conflict with the cattle raisers turned into an issue for the whole Tribe. Many Seminole felt they were being ignored and left out of the success of the program. They thought that the successful cattle raisers should help the unsuccessful ones so that they too would be successful. Friction between tribal members on this issue almost disrupted the entire cattle program.

After World War II, housing on the Seminole reservations changed. A type of building found all over southern Florida, known as the cement block structure, or CBS, was built on the reservations. This type of building, which is "hurricane proof," was required by the state because the area is frequently hit by hurricanes. CBSs are ranch-style houses consisting of one floor with two or three bedrooms, a kitchen, a bathroom, and a living-dining room. Attached to the house is a breezeway that serves as a carport and beyond that a utility room, which sometimes includes a washing machine. The houses have interior running water and a sewage system.

WHAT'S IN A NAME?

Perhaps the most obvious impact of the Seminole on the non-Indian world is in the many Florida place names derived from their languages. Tallahassee, the state capital, is Muskogee for "old town." Lake Okeechobee gets its name from a Mikasuki word meaning "big water." The present day town and county of Alachua have the same name as an 18th-century Seminole village.

Some Florida place names are probably English translations of Muskogee words that were too difficult for non-Indians to pronounce. Crystal River is very likely the English rendering of *Wewakiahakee*, or "clear water." Fish-eating Creek, which flows into Lake Okeechobee, is thought to be the translation of the Seminole word meaning "the stream where fish are eaten."

The names of several Seminole leaders have been given to towns. Emathla is named for Charley Emathla, a Seminole leader who agreed to move to Oklahoma. The town of Micanopy honors the Seminole chief Micanopy, who joined Osceola in resisting removal to the West. Osceola himself has had both a town and a county named in his memory.

A glance at a map of Florida shows many delightful names derived from Seminole languages: Okaloacoochee Slough; Pahokee; Chattahochee; Withlacoochee; Yeehaw; and Loxahatchee, among others. Lake Miccosukee is an alternative spelling of Mikasuki, one of the languages spoken by the Seminole and the name of the organized tribe of Indians living along the Tamiami Trail.

Some reminders of the earlier Indians of Florida are still around today. The Caloosahatchee River is derived from the Calusa tribe that lived in southern Florida when the Spanish arrived. The cities of Pensacola and Apalachicola bear the names of two early southeastern tribes. The first reference to Miami comes from Spanish explorers who wrote about a lake that the early Florida Indians called *Mayaimi* or *Maymi*. Translated, this word means "very large," and the Indians who spoke of it were referring to Lake Okeechobee.

When the Seminole moved from their traditional chickees into CBSs, they began a new way of life. There were no beds, tables, or chairs in the chickees. At night, the Indians had previously unrolled mats or pads on which to sleep. They sat directly on the chickee platform and hung their belongings on palmetto branches. Now the Indians had to buy furniture for the first time. Their new houses had closets, and the Indians had to learn how to use them. At first many people simply piled their clothes on the floors of the closets, but they soon discovered the use of clothes hangers.

Seminole women inspect a cement block structure (CBS) at Dania Reservation in 1956. CBSs were expressly designed to withstand the hurricanes that occasionally brought severe destruction to southern Florida.

The women were used to preparing foods in blackened pots over an open fire. Now they had to learn how to cook on a stove, use an oven, and remember to turn the burners off when they were finished cooking. They were used to storing food in open baskets and had to learn about refrigerators and to keep the refrigerator door closed.

The state and county sent home economists to teach the women how to work in their new kitchens. The Seminole learned how to cook with new equipment—pans and bowls, rolling pins, egg beaters, and scrapers. The teachers were amazed at the ability of the women to remember complex operations. Because almost none of them had learned to read, they could not refer to cookbooks or other written instructions. Instead they watched the demonstrations intently and learned to duplicate operations in a very short time, often after watching only once.

A Seminole woman prepares frybread, a traditional Indian food, in her modern kitchen. To retain their culture, the Indians combined their customs with those of the non-Indian society in which they also functioned.

The home economists also taught about sanitation: how to use a vacuum cleaner, mop, and broom; how to clean sinks and stoves with various cleansers; and how to sanitize toilets and drains. All these activities were introduced so that the Seminole would know how to live in and maintain their new houses.

Despite the fact that they could not read and spoke little English, the women were able to purchase processed foods and household items from grocery stores in town. They could locate the different brands of food or the cleansers the home economists had used through their visual memory, which enabled them to recognize labels by color and picture and served them as reading would serve others.

The CBSs had many modern features, but not everybody on the reservations wanted to live in them. For one thing, they were expensive. In addition, in the heat and humidity of the Florida summer they became very hot because they were completely enclosed—unlike the chickees, whose sides could be opened to catch the breezes. Consequently, the Seminole Tribe of Florida, with help from the federal agency at Hollywood, developed plans for new housing in the mid-1960s. These dwellings combined the best features of the CBS with the traditional chickee.

The new housing is referred to as self-help housing because each family interested in acquiring it is required to contribute labor. Family members help with projects such as painting and carpentry. Plumbing and electrical work that must be approved by the state are built by professionals. This type of housing is much cheaper than a CBS.

The self-help housing consists of several structures for each family, an arrangement that is similiar to the traditional camp of chickees. Three separate buildings house the sleeping quarters, the kitchen-dining area, and the bathroom. The kitchen contains an electric stove, modern sink, refrigerator, cabinets, and space for a table and chairs.

Each unit is built on a poured-cement base and made of wood. The interiors are not completely enclosed as in the CBS; instead, there are almost continuous windows on all sides, at a height of about four feet. The windows are screened and can be closed against rain and cool weather. The large windows allow a free flow of air, just as the structure of the traditional chickees did, so the housing is far more comfortable in hot weather than the CBS. The units are attractive, and the cement floors make cleaning easy. The space between the units also creates a small courtyard where children can play under the watchful eye of adults.

As the form of housing in the 20th century changed from chickees to CBS homes to self-help housing, the form of the family changed also. The extended family is now rare, and the tendency is clearly toward the nuclear family—a man, woman, and their children, without other relatives. This trend is stronger among those on the coast and those who live in CBS or self-help housing. There is usually less room for extra relatives in these new kinds of houses, unlike in the traditional camp, where the family could simply construct another chickee for incoming kinfolk. Furthermore, married couples today want to set up their own home. This is the ideal of the outside society, and it has become the ideal of the Seminole.

Family structure has changed not only because of the move into different housing. Contact with the non-Indian world has resulted in changes in occupation and a greater desire for material goods and education. Parents want their children to have things they did not have, and they also want more for themselves. ▲

The committee that drafted the constitution of the Seminole Tribe of Florida in August 1957.

THE
SEMINOLE
TODAY

Today the Seminole people make their living in a variety of ways: working for commercial fruit and vegetable growers, doing road work, raising cattle, working for the Seminole Tribe of Florida and the Seminole agency, selling arts and crafts, and operating stores. Some people do not have much cash income and receive welfare benefits instead.

Work for the vegetable and fruit growers off the reservation continues to be an important source of income. Large food-processing corporations such as the Campbell Soup Company and Del Monte employ many farm laborers, and both men and women find seasonal employment there. But except for Hollywood Reservation, the tribal lands are too remote from centers where jobs might be available. This prevents most employment that would require commuting to cities. For jobs off the reservation, people must either find work close by or live near the work, which can be expensive unless arrange-

ments can be made with friends or relatives. However, many commercial growers provide living quarters for the people they hire as seasonal agricultural laborers.

Since World War II, increased opportunities for employment on the reservations have arisen. One has been work on the roads that were constructed across reservation territory. Road maintenance work on Big Cypress and Brighton reservations is a source of employment for some Indians. Men who had learned to operate the large road-building equipment, such as bulldozers and graders, in earlier decades have earned good incomes from this work. They enjoy not only the work itself but also the respect they receive from other Seminoles. Road work is constant in south Florida; the damage caused by heavy rains and the unstable foundation of the roads means that repairs are frequently needed. Some men have obtained positions on road crews off the reservations. These experiences, like those with cattle raising, have created new self-confidence as well as provided a good income for the people who held those jobs.

The cattle-raising program continues on the reservations. However, on a daily basis the industry is not a major source of employment. There are periods of intensive labor, such as when the cattle are rounded up for shipment or for vaccination, but most of the time the Indians do not have to work in the fields or holding pens.

The Seminole Tribe of Florida itself is a major employer of office staff such as secretaries and various administrative aides. The tribal arts and crafts store and Indian Village Enterprise, important tourist attractions, also employ Indians. The Indian Village Enterprise is a reconstructed traditional Seminole village that tourists pay to visit. Most tribal employment, however, goes to residents of Hollywood Reservation because the headquarters and stores are located there and most of the admin-

The souvenir shop at Okallee Village, a reconstructed Seminole village and tourist attraction at Hollywood Reservation.

istration of the Tribe is conducted there. The federal agency office for the Seminole, also at Hollywood, hires people to do similar types of office work.

Men and women continue to receive income from handcrafts, making traditional dolls, garments, baskets, and carvings. The older women of the Tribe make most of these items. They are sold at the Tribe's arts and crafts store or in stores and gas stations near the reservations. Various tourist centers in Florida contract with the Tribe's craftspeople for quantities of craft items. Because tourists now visit Florida all year instead of only in winter, crafts have become a year-round source of income for many families.

The Seminole practice a certain amount of small-scale retailing in stores at various locations on the reservations. The merchants maintain a small inventory of packaged goods for people who are far from supermarkets. Since the late 1950s, when electricity was brought to the reservations and refrigeration became possible, people at Brighton and Big Cypress have sold cold drinks. The income from these sales is slight. However, managing even a small food store is an experience that develops skills and confidence. The stores provide young people with a place to socialize as well as to buy such universally favorite snacks as soft drinks and potato chips.

Some Indians receive welfare benefits, and those older people who have been employed receive Social Security payments. Indians are eligible for these state and federal funds on the same basis as any other U.S. citizens. Because many Seminoles do not have much schooling and the jobs that are available to them do not pay well, Indian incomes are substantially lower than those in the non-Indian society. The Seminole make up part of the difference by growing some of their food and by hunting. By law they have the right to hunt on reservations at any time of year, and they do not need state hunting licenses.

Despite the variety of opportunities for employment, many Seminole are underemployed. This is because their levels of education and training are too low for jobs in today's economy in Florida, and also because the Indians, especially those on the interior reservations, often live too far away from employment possiblities. The Seminole help one another so that no one in need is neglected.

In the 1980s the Seminole Tribe of Florida, in its continuous search for additional sources of income, took a new and somewhat controversial step that was vigorously debated both among the tribespeople and within the state. They decided to conduct bingo operations, first at Hollywood Reservation and then at the other reservations. The Tribe arranged for the construction of large buildings, each spacious enough for several thousand players; the one at Big Cypress is described as being "like a misplaced aircraft hangar." Like casinos in places such as Atlantic City and

Las Vegas, the bingo halls attract people from considerable distances, some of whom come on chartered buses. The Tribe hopes to raise large amounts of money through the bingo operations.

Because Hollywood Reservation is closer than the other Seminole reservations to major centers of non-Indian population, the employment situation and way of living there are different from those at the other reservations. The people at Hollywood are not only better educated but also more integrated into the general Florida population. They live near a variety of employment opportunities, and they hold jobs in manufacturing and other industrial enterprises as well as selling at stores in nearby shopping centers. Buses serve the area, which makes transportation much easier.

Because of the political and economic importance of Hollywood Reservation and its more sophisticated way of life, the people who live there are viewed with some envy by those who live at Brighton and Big Cypress. However, Indians on the interior reservations say they do not want to live at Hollywood. They feel the people there have lost all their traditional ways, and they find the pace of life at Hollywood unpleasant. Much as they want the material goods money will buy, many Seminole are still unwilling to change their traditional way of life for the stresses of living and working at or near Hollywood.

Notwithstanding the variations between the residents of Hollywood, Brighton, and Big Cypress reservations, the way of life of all Seminole has changed in the latter part of the 20th century. For instance, the Seminole today get most of their food from grocery stores, including many processed foods. Their eating habits are similar to those of other Floridians. There is an especially high consumption of soft drinks. The amount of sugar in these beverages has contributed to the Indians' high incidence of tooth decay.

There are three foods the Seminole often eat that are not eaten by non-Indians: sofki, frybread, and swamp cabbage. Sofki is the traditional vegetable drink of southeastern Indians. The Seminole make it with mashed or pounded corn that is boiled in water. This thick drink may also contain mashed pumpkin or tomatoes, but the most common form is made only with corn. Many Seminole drink it warm or cooled with meals instead of milk or water. The people at Hollywood Reservation drink sofki less often than those on the other reservations.

Frybread is a familiar dish for most Indian communities in the United States. The Seminole prepare it in much the same way that Indians in other regions do. They combine wheat flour, salt, baking powder, and shortening then pat the dough into a large pancake and fry it. The bread resembles a large biscuit that has been fried instead of baked.

A Miccosukee woman demonstrates how to make frybread at an Indian village specially constructed to show tourists the daily life of the Seminole.

Swamp cabbage is actually the inner part of the sabal palmetto bud. It is known to non-Indians as hearts of palm. Because of the work involved in obtaining it, swamp cabbage is quite expensive on the market. Most of the palmetto is inedible, and the entire tree is destroyed when it is topped to get the young, tender inside portion. The Seminole eat it raw—it tastes something like celery—or cooked, boiled, or lightly sautéed. The sabal palmetto is abundant on the interior reservations.

In addition to these traditional foods, wild game, especially deer, adds to the Seminole diet. For special occasions the Indians will slaughter a steer.

Before the 1960s, men and women on Brighton and Big Cypress reservations still wore some traditional items of clothing. The women continued to wear long skirts banded with colorful strips that were inlaid with patchwork, a short cape over their shoulders, and many strings of beads. A few elderly men continued to wear the traditional kilt, but most men began to wear blue jeans and shirts.

In the 1960s, girls and young women started wearing jeans and shorts. On Hollywood Reservation these practices were accepted, but the more traditional Indians on other reservations felt that such dress was immodest. Today, young Seminole women dress in the same manner as women in the general Florida society.

The older women often still wear the traditional long skirts.

Only the older women continue to dress their hair in the manner that was popular in the early years of the 20th century. The women brushed their hair up toward the crown of their head and then combed it over and under a form similar to a hatbrim so that they created

A Seminole mother arranges her daughter's hair. Seminole women have for many years worn a unique hairstyle. The long hair is combed up toward the crown of the head and then over and under a form similar to a hat brim. This custom has been disappearing because women do not have the time it takes to arrange such an elaborate hairstyle.

a type of sunshade with their own hair. Although long black hair is still highly desirable, few women today wish to spend the time required to arrange their long hair in the old way.

The Seminole find entertainment from the same sources as many other U.S. citizens. Seminole of all ages watch television. Although many of the older people do not understand English, they nevertheless enjoy watching the programs. Before power lines were run to the interior reservations, the Seminole used battery-operated radios to hear their favorite music. The Indians enjoyed country-and-western and rock music.

Very occasionally, adults go to town to see a movie. High school girls and boys play softball or basketball on the reservations and in leagues in nearby towns. The younger children play on the elementary school playgrounds on and off the reservations. Everyone still enjoys fishing and catching turtles.

Most families own or have access to a car, and people of all ages enjoy trips to town. Those with regular employment can afford good cars; the others have learned to repair old cars. The men are very competent at renovating their old cars. Because many are unable to read and speak little English, they have learned about cars by working on them. Sometimes they take various parts from broken vehicles and combine them to make one car that runs. As a gesture of good will, the state of Florida gives the Seminole special free license plates with the legend "Seminole Indian."

James Billie, chairperson of the Seminole Tribe of Florida, in 1987.

Public holidays such as Independence Day bring the Seminole into town to view parades and other festivities. Sometimes Indians participate in these programs, but activities in association with non-Indians are still quite rare.

One activity of the Seminole has attracted non-Indians. Since the 1960s, the Seminole Tribe of Florida has held several powwows. Originally, the Tribe wanted to create a celebration for themselves alone, but publicity about the powwows spread and outsiders began to attend. The three reservations take turns hosting the event, which includes athletic events and other contests, arts and crafts exhibitions, and a big feast of traditional and nontraditional foods. The people of the sponsoring reservation do most of the work involved in running the event, but it is not considered labor because the event has become so popular. Powwows are held during the summer when school is out and when there are more tourists to attend. When the powwow is held at Hollywood, the reservation most accessible to tourists, the tourist dollar is especially sought out. At that reservation Seminole men demonstrate alligator wrestling. The Tribe's arts and crafts store is at Hollywood and offers many souvenirs made by Seminole craftspeople and members of other Indian tribes.

The family is still extremely important to the Seminole. Although in the 1980s the nuclear family is more common, many families still include relatives other than a pair of parents and their children. Often the wife's mother, or perhaps the wife's sister, lives with the family. This pattern is common be-

At the wedding of Chief Tony Tommy and Edna John Osceola, the guests performed the Green Corn Dance after the ceremony. Marriages, once formalized agreements between families, are now usually church or civil ceremonies and are decided upon by the two individuals involved.

cause of the continuing matrilineal clan organization. Clan affiliation is still recognized among the Seminole. The people all know their clans, and it is rare even today that anyone will marry someone from the same clan. After the long period of hostilities with the U.S. Army in the mid-1800s, some clans became extinct. As clans died out it became increasingly difficult to maintain rules that required marriage outside one's own clan. Often there were no suitable marriage partners. In the early part of the 20th century intraclan marriages were still highly disapproved of but today no one is shocked by them, although they are still considered undesirable.

Marriage between Seminoles and whites or blacks occurred occasionally. These mixed marriages were more disapproved of than marriages within a clan, but by World War II the Seminole's attitudes had changed, and there were children of mixed parentage living on all of the reservations and in towns nearby. Those children and the non-Indian parent were, and continue to be, accepted without question by the rest of the Seminole community.

Today a marriage ceremony is usually a church or civil affair. The traditional arranged marriage, which was formalized only by agreement and gift-giving between the families involved, is dying out. One reason is that many Indians are church members who feel pressured to conform to the traditions of the church. Another reason is that the state requires proof of marriage for certain financial and legal matters, such as social security, tax determination, adoption, and inheritance. Florida has recognized traditional Indian unions as a form of common-law marriage, but state officials have been urging the Indians to have civil ceremonies. One traditional form of Indian marriage the state has never recognized is polygyny: a living arrangement in which a man has two or more wives.

A newly wed couple may still move in with the woman's parents, forming a matrilineally extended family. But increasingly, the newlyweds will try to find a home of their own. Very few people now live in chickees. Although there are mixed marriages on all of the reservations, many such couples prefer to live off the reservation because the non-Indian partner may feel somewhat uneasy in the Indian community.

Married Seminole in today's society want children. If they can have none of their own, they often ask to raise a relative's child. The Seminole regard foster parenting as a logical way of helping out, especially if the relative has financial difficulties and a large family. The foster parents do not legally adopt a child. An agreement is simply made between two sets of parents. The result is usually to everyone's benefit: The childless couple gets to raise a child and the other parents get relief from economic stress. The children are always told the facts of the situation, and they may visit their real parents from time to time.

All Seminole babies are born in hospitals today, and expectant mothers receive the same kind of care available to women in the general population: examinations, medicine, and vitamin supplements. During pregnancy, women go to private doctors or to doctors under contract to the BIA. In addition, the county public health nurse is an important source of information and care.

If a baby is a girl, her mother or aunt will pierce her ears shortly after she is brought home from the hospital. At one time, boys' ears were pierced too, but that practice is no longer observed. After four months, the baby receives a haircut and the fingernails are trimmed. In keeping with Seminole tradition, the mother will save the hair and nail clippings to give to the child in adulthood. This is an old custom that is still common at Big Cypress and among the Tamiami Indians, but it is dying out at Hollywood and Brighton. Traditionally, during the first four months of a child's life, the mother lived with the baby in a separate chickee. Now that most young families live in modern housing, the mother and baby stay in the house with the father and any other children. Many young people today do not even know about the old custom.

Soon after birth, babies receive English names. This is necessary because a child must have a first and last name on its birth certificate. Traditionally, Seminoles had only one name that was given to them on the fourth day after birth. This Indian name was suggested by an aged person. Boys were given new names at a Green Corn Dance when they were about 12 years old. Children now use their father's last name in addition to their English given name, which is usually non-Indian because some sounds in the Seminole languages do not have corresponding letters in the English alphabet. They may also have an Indian name that is given to them during their first week of life. This name will not appear on the birth certificate, but parents and close relatives may use it instead of the English name. On Hollywood Reservation use of Indian names has died off for the most part.

Children are usually cared for by their mothers. Today, however, women frequently work outside the home and must rely on others to help them. Grandparents often care for children, but parents usually depend on their older children to help with younger ones, to a degree not known in the general population.

During the day Seminole children go to school. There is an Indian Day School at Big Cypress for grades one through four, after which the children go to public school off the reservation. The Tamiami Indians also have an elementary school on their reservation. Children at Brighton and Hollywood attend public school off the reservation from the beginning.

During the summer, children may attend programs established both to advance them academically and to acquaint them with aspects of the general society with which they may not be fa-

Students at Ahfachkee School, an elementary school at Big Cypress Reservation.

miliar. Teachers work on general etiquette and behavior, hygiene, English vocabulary and pronunciation, and arts and crafts. Summer school is regarded as fun by many children. They especially enjoy using paints, crayons, colored paper, pipe cleaners, and other art materials. They also like summer school because their academic work is not graded and there are no report cards. Recorded music accompanies many of their activities, as well.

Adults rarely punish children. Babies are loved and fondled almost constantly. Parents expect teenage children to think for themselves and rarely tell them what to do. However, some Sem-

inole believe that too little guidance is given to children today. Part of the problem is that the older children who attend schools off the reservations are in situations that their parents have never experienced. The parents find it difficult to understand the modern, non-Indian ways with which their children are growing up. They are often unable to give appropriate advice to their children, and when a young person gets in trouble, there is no one to consult.

There are now many Seminoles with high school diplomas, and a number have obtained associate's degrees from a community college. More and more students are receiving both associate's and bachelor's degrees. These graduates are setting new examples for the next generation.

Educated Indians who return to the reservations can be an important influence on young people. Unfortunately, only Indians from Hollywood Reservation usually return after completing their schooling; educated Indians from the interior reservations prefer to live in towns or at Hollywood and return to reservations only to visit. There are various reasons for this, but the most important is that there are greater employment opportunities off the interior reservations. Furthermore, life on the interior reservations is considered boring by the young people because of the lack of social and intellectual opportunities. The educated Indians are also viewed with jealousy or disrespect by their peers on the reservations. Educated Indians will live at Hollywood because the residents are better educated and more sophisticated than those on the interior reservations. It is also located near other communities that have numerous employment and leisure-time opportunities.

Reaction to school often depends on a person's home environment. Many Indian households do not provide a home atmosphere that is conducive to study. There is often no place to study without interruption, and there are few books. Some children have felt that their parents do not care about their work in school because the adults cannot help with homework and do not ask about the children's progress. Parents do care, but they themselves have not had the education their children are getting, and thus do not have the knowledge to help.

Parents who have never attended public schools are unable to help when their children have problems in school. It is frequently difficult for the Seminole children to make friends with their schoolmates because their lives are quite different from those of non-Indian children. On some reservations, especially Big Cypress, the public school is far from home, and children may spend two hours a day just riding the school bus. The dependency on bus transport makes it difficult, if not impossible, for Seminole youths to participate in after-school activities such as sports and social clubs, which would help them get to know their fellow students. In addition, they are unable to make good use of school facilities such as the library because they must get on the bus as soon as classes are over.

Many Seminole adults believe that the public schools do not acknowledge the importance of their Indian students' cultural and linguistic traditions. Consequently, they are not alarmed when children drop out of school and do not make efforts to persuade them to stay. Some parents, especially on the interior reservations, do not understand that the education provided by the public schools will benefit their children and make them employable. Those who live on Hollywood Reservation have had far more experience with the Florida school system, and they see that schooling is necessary to obtain many jobs. They do make every effort to keep their sons and daughters in school and even encourage them to continue their education at nearby junior colleges.

Education has brought change to the Seminole, and so has Christianity. More Seminole converted to Christianity in the second half of the 20th century, following the example set by certain influential Indians. A few Seminole have been ordained as Baptist ministers, and churches have been built on the reservations. However, not all Seminole have converted. Some families were divided by differing allegiances when some members joined Christian churches whereas others remained faithful to old beliefs. But the Seminole are very tolerant of individual variation, and the differences of reli-

Seminole Indians attend church services at Big Cypress Reservation. Church-related activities provide many Seminole with opportunities for worship and socializing.

For more than 200 years the Seminole have survived as a tribe by adapting to change without giving up their traditional ways entirely. The preservation of their customs has helped the Seminole maintain a strong sense of identity as a distinct and proud people.

gious persuasion never affected families to the extent of causing friction.

The Seminole who have been ordained or trained as lay preachers may conduct services in one of the Seminole languages or in English. Church services are good opportunities for announcements because many people may be reached at one time. Church events that take place on the interior reservations often provide a change of pace during periods of inactivity and allow people an opportunity for general socializing. Although not all Seminole are members of Christian churches, most do participate in community events held at churches, such as Sunday night suppers. Activities for children are also held on church premises.

Christian tales and references have permeated the traditional mythology, becoming so intertwined that it is difficult to separate the older beliefs from the new. The Seminole find no conflict in merging traditional beliefs with Christian doctrine. The greatest difficulty for the remaining practitioners of the old ways is to find young people willing to spend the time and effort to learn about them.

There is very little left of the old religious philosophies. The last generation of shamans died without leaving many disciples. Observers believe that there may still be some shamanistic practices on the Tamiami Trail, but native religious activity at the other reservations is confined to certain medical practices with native plants. What the aged people remember of any older religious belief system is so mingled with what they have learned of Christianity that little of the older belief can be untangled.

The traditional Green Corn Dance is no longer held regularly, and when it is held, many Seminole feel that the ceremony of today is a travesty of the old, sacred ceremony. For several decades it has not been performed anywhere except among the Tamiami Indians, and these performances are reported to have been occasions for excessive drinking. Many Seminole who have become Christianized would like to see the ceremony halted altogether. Other Seminole remember that the Green Corn Dance was once a very solemn and sacred ritual of purification and thanksgiving, and they would like to see it return in its original form, as a renewal ceremony cleansed of its new association with alcohol. However, as the Indians are drawn into the ways of the larger population, all forms of the Green Corn Dance seem likely to disappear. Other rituals and concerns will probably replace it.

The broadcast media have been very important in developing the Seminole's ideas about the world. Battery-operated radios are popular on all reservations, and television has brought not only the sounds but also the sights of the outside world to young and old. The fact that the television view of the world might not always be strictly accurate or representative is quite beside the point. Soap operas and movies, as well as newscasts and sports, have familiarized the isolated Seminole with many facets of urban life they have never seen.

The Seminole who settled at Brighton and those at the coastal reservation, Hollywood, are the most acculturated. They have more contact with non-Indians and participate more in the customs of the non-Indian world. There are more English speakers among those groups, and more of them have been to school. Least acculturated are those who have organized as the Miccosukee Tribe. The people at Big Cypress are somewhere between these two extremes. Some speak English fluently, and a few have graduated from high school. The inevitable result of education has been increased facility in communicating with outsiders, increased employment on the outside, and an accelerated loss of traditional, tribal ways.

But the older people have not had this education. At Brighton and Big Cypress, they often prefer their restful, quiet life. They visit Hollywood, but after a while are glad to return home. The tempo of their day is leisurely. There is always time to stop and visit with friends and family, and that is the way the days pass. ▲

BIBLIOGRAPHY

Bartram, William. *The Travels of William Bartram*. New Haven: Yale University Press, 1958.

Capron, Louis. "Florida's Emerging Seminoles." *National Geographic*, Nov. 1969, 716–733.

Garbarino, Merwyn S. *Big Cypress: A Changing Seminole Community*. New York: Holt, Rinehart & Winston, 1972.

Glenn, James L. *My Work Among the Florida Seminoles*. Orlando: University Presses of Florida, 1982.

Hudson, Charles. *The Southeastern Indians*. Knoxville: University of Tennessee Press, 1976.

Jones, Kenneth M. *War with the Seminoles: 1835–1842*. New York: Franklin Watts, 1975.

McReynolds, Edwin C. *Seminoles*. Norman: University of Oklahoma Press, 1972.

Sturtevant, William C. "A Seminole Medicine Maker." In *In the Company of Man*, edited by Joseph B. Casagrande. New York: Harper & Row, 1957.

Tebeau, C. W. *Florida's Last Frontier*. Coral Gables, FL: University of Miami Press, 1957.

THE SEMINOLE AT A GLANCE

TRIBES *Seminole Tribe of Florida*
Miccosukee Tribe

CULTURE AREA *Southeastern United States*

GEOGRAPHY *members of several southeastern tribes and fugitive slaves took refuge in northern Florida, where they formed the Seminole tribe; currently southern Florida*

LINGUISTIC FAMILY *Muskhogean (divisions: Muskogee, Mikasuki)*

TRADITIONAL ECONOMY *hunting, foraging, horticulture*

CURRENT POPULATION *(1985 figures) Seminole Tribe of Florida: approximately 1400; Miccosukee Tribe: approximately 500*

FEDERAL STATUS *recognized tribe. Most of the members of the Seminole Tribe of Florida live on three reservations: Big Cypress, Brighton, and Hollywood. Most of the members of the Miccosukee Tribe live on the Miccosukee Reservation or along the Tamiami Trail.*

GLOSSARY

acculturation The process by which one culture changes and adapts to the dominant culture it confronts.

agent; Indian agent A person appointed by the Bureau of Indian Affairs to supervise U.S. government programs on a reservation and/or in a specific region; after 1908 the title "superintendent" replaced "agent."

annuity Compensation for land and/or resources based on terms of a treaty or other agreement between the United States and an individual tribe; consisted of goods, services, and cash given to the tribe every year for a specified period.

black drink An herbal drink used by tribes throughout the Southeast to induce vomiting as part of a purification ritual.

Bureau of Indian Affairs (BIA) A U.S. government agency established in 1824 and assigned to the Department of the Interior in 1849. Originally intended to manage trade and other relations with Indians and especially to supervise tribes on reservations, the BIA is now involved in programs that encourage Indians to manage their own affairs and improve their educational opportunities and general social and economic well-being.

cement block structure (CBS) Hurricane-proof housing constructed of cement blocks; used throughout southern Florida from the 1940s through the present.

chickee An open-sided structure built on a raised platform and covered by a thatched roof; the traditional housing of the Seminole adapted to the southern Florida environment.

clan A multigenerational group having a shared identity, organization, and property, based on belief in descent from a common ancestor. Because clan members consider themselves closely related, marriage within the clan is strictly prohibited. Seminole clan membership is determined by matrilineal descent.

culture The learned behavior of human beings; nonbiological, socially taught activities; the way of life of a given group of people.

Everglades An area of marshlands approximately 40 miles square in southern Florida.

extended family Several generations of people connected by kinship and marriage who live with or near each other; includes parents, children, grandparents, aunts and uncles, and other relatives.

Green Corn Dance Celebration of purification, forgiveness, and thanksgiving held annually when the new crop of corn ripened.

horticulture Production of food using human muscle power and simple hand tools to plant and harvest domesticated crops. Horticulture is commonly women's work. Agriculture, which requires the power of draft animals and larger tools such as plows, is usually men's work.

hummock An area of dry land suitable for housing and horticulture that rises slightly above the swampland of southern Florida; also *hammock*.

hunting-and-gathering; foraging An economic system based on the collection of food by hunting wild animals, fishing, and gathering wild plant foods; the most ancient of human ways of obtaining the necessities of life.

Indian Reorganization Act 1934 federal law that ended the policy of allotting plots of land to individuals and provided for political and economic development of reservation communities.

Indian Removal Act 1830 federal law that authorized the relocation of eastern Indian tribes to new lands west of the Mississippi River.

matrilineal; matrilineality A principle of descent by which kinship is traced through female ancestors; the basis for Seminole clan membership.

matrilocal residence A tradition in which a newly married couple lives with or near the wife's mother's family.

medicine bag A pouch containing objects of spiritual and practical value used in rituals.

Miccosukee Tribe One of two federally recognized organizations of Seminole Indians. Incorporated in 1962, the Tribe is predominantly made up of Indians living on or near the Tamiami Trail.

Mikasuki One of the languages of the Florida Seminole; a language within the Muskhogean family.

Muskhogean The family of languages spoken by most Indian tribes of southeastern North America.

Muskogee One of the languages of the Florida Seminole; a language within the Muskhogean family.

nuclear family A family unit consisting of a mother, father, and one or more of their children.

polygyny A form of marriage in which a man has two or more wives at one time.

powwow An Indian social gathering that includes feasting, dancing, rituals, and arts and crafts displays, to which other Indian groups as well as non-Indians are now often invited.

removal policy National policy of 1830 calling for the sale of all Indian land in the states and the migration of Indians from eastern and southern states to and resettlement in a segregated, exclusively Indian territory (Kansas and Oklahoma). Those Indians who remained in the east came under state laws.

reservation A tract of land set aside by treaty for the occupation and use of Indians; also called a reserve. Some reservations were for an entire tribe; many others were for unaffiliated Indians.

self-help housing Federal housing for reservation Indians that requires the residents to help in the construction. The Seminole self-help housing style, based on that of the traditional chickee, consists of three separate structures, each with continuous windows on all sides to allow for maximum air flow.

Seminole Tribe of Florida One of the two federally recognized organizations of Seminole Indians. Incorporated in 1957, the Tribe is governed by a constitution and is headed by a council and board of directors.

shaman A person who has special powers to call on various spirits to solve problems, heal the sick, or ensure success in acquiring food or in other essential activities.

sofki The traditional vegetable drink of the southeastern Indians; commonly made from mashed corn boiled in water.

squatters People who occupy land without having legal title to it.

sweathouse An airtight hut in which rituals are held. The steam produced by pouring water over heated rocks helps a person achieve a condition of spiritual purification.

taboo A forbidden practice or act thought to anger or upset the supernatural world; people who committed a taboo act were required to take appropriate actions to restore harmony.

treaty A contract negotiated between representatives of the United States and one or more Indian tribes. Treaties dealt with surrender of political independence, peaceful relations, land sales and payments for them, boundaries, and related matters.

tribe A type of society consisting of several or many separate communities united by kinship and such social units as clans, religious organizations, economic and political institutions, a common culture, and language. Tribes are generally characterized by economic and political equality, and thus lack social classes and authoritative chiefs.

trust land Land set aside and controlled by the U.S. government for use by Indians.

wampum A medium of exchange, or type of money, consisting of beads made from white and purple parts of clam and oyster shells. From the Algonquian word *wampumpeag*, meaning white (bead) strings.

INDEX

PICTURE CREDITS

MERWYN S. GARBARINO is a professor of anthropology at the University of Illinois. She received her Ph.D. from Northwestern University and has performed field work on reservations in Florida, the Northern Plains, the Great Lakes region, and with urban Indians in Chicago. She has published four books, including *Big Cypress: A Changing Seminole Community*, and her articles have appeared in numerous journals.

FRANK W. PORTER III, General Editor of INDIANS OF NORTH AMERICA, is Director of the Chelsea House Foundation for American Indian Studies. He holds a B.A., M.A., and Ph.D. from the University of Maryland. He has done extensive research concerning the Indians of Maryland and Delaware and is the author of numerous articles on their history, archaeology, geography, and ethnography. He was formerly Director of the Maryland Commission on Indian Affairs and American Indian Research and Resource Institute, Gettysburg, Pennsylvania, and he has received grants from the Delaware Humanities Forum, the Maryland Committee for the Humanities, the Ford Foundation, and the National Endowment for the Humanities, among others. Dr. Porter is the author of *The Bureau of Indian Affairs* in the Chelsea House KNOW YOUR GOVERNMENT series.